OLD WOMEN AND OTHER STRANGERS

ESSAYS

LINDA C. WISNIEWSKI

Catherine Street Press
Cover photograph by Matt Wisniewski, www.mattw.us

ISBN 979-8-218-42488-6

CONTENTS

Part I

A MID-CENTURY CHILDHOOD

BROWNIE'S MEXICAN HOTS 7
ORCHID IN THE SNOW 13
MATTERS OF FACT 19
THE HARTWICK COLLEGE MAN 23
HOW CAN I KEEP FROM WALKING 27
REID HILL MEMORIES 33
MRS. BROWN'S TEARS 37
PINE LAKE 41
MY GRANDFATHER'S EAR 47
LIFESAVER 53

Part II

CONNECTIONS

OCTOBER DANCE 59
LOVE, FORGIVENESS, FOOTBALL 63
YOU HAVE TO EAT LUNCH 67
A CONNECTING THREAD 73
BREAD ON THE GRASS 79
STREET STORIES 83
THE DARNING EGG 89

Part III

OTHERS

OLD WOMEN AND OTHER STRANGERS 95
WALK IN WELCOME 101
STOP KISSING ME 107
LIGHTEN UP 111
BULLIES, THEN AND NOW 117
DANGER BOY 121

Part IV
HEARTSTRINGS
WE CAME FOR TOAST 129
A LIFETIME LATER 133
THIS IS A MOMENT OF SUFFERING 137
TEMPORARY TEARS 141
TWISTED 145
I WANT TO GO HOME 149

Part V
DISCOVERIES
FRESH OFF THE BOAT 155
NOTES FROM AN AMERICAN ISLAND 161
THEY CALL THEMSELVES INDIANS 165
LIBRETTO DECAFFEINATO 171
REDISCOVERING THE OLD COUNTRY 175
THIRTY-TWO WORDS FOR PEACE 181
WIDE OPEN SPACES 187

Part VI
SPIRIT DRAW NEAR
MADONNA WITH SCARS 191
LATE BLESSING 197
NOTES ON TRANSCENDENCE 205
FAITH IN THE FAMILY ROOM 209

Part VII
SHE WRITES
WHY I STILL WRITE 215
CLASS OF REBELS 219
WRITE ME HOME 223

Acknowledgments 227

PART I

A MID-CENTURY CHILDHOOD

BROWNIE'S MEXICAN HOTS

Some days, only a hot dog will do. A hot sausage in a bun with pickle relish on top, filling my mouth as I bite into it, bursting its casing with salty juices, relieving a deeply held craving. A craving born in my childhood, a craving for attention, love, approval and affirmation from a man who was mostly unable to give me those things. My father.

On Saturday, March 13th, 1954, a tiny square on page twelve of the *Amsterdam Evening Recorder* held an ad for Brownie's Lunch at 26 East Main Street. The ad shared the page with others for Boggie's Fourth Ward Hotel, Klub Aloha, The Friendly Tavern, DePaul's Italian American Restaurant, the G.L.F. Farm Store, Mohawk Cleaners and Dyers, Kaye's Furniture Store and St. Patrick's Night Carnival of Joy. There was barely room on page twelve for the Hospital Record of births and the actual news: "Red Cross Launches Week-Long Canvass," "Guy Park Ave. Petitions Urge Assessment Reforms," "Deal Asks Community Support for Industrial Expansion Drive."

My hometown had business and news enough to fill a full-sized print newspaper, though the last headline foreshadowed what was to come. The rug mills, where most of the town's citizens, including my parents, made enough money to buy a small home, pay for parochial school tuition and give to the church, were about to leave town for cheaper labor in the South and later overseas.

In that world, there was no Brownie's Lunch for me without my father. My little sister Judy and I would sit quietly across from him in a booth, as we learned to sit quietly everywhere. After school, he would take us here for one of his favorite treats: Brownie's hotdogs.

"Can't you cook anything but fish?" asks the man in the ad, wearing a sleeveless t-shirt and leaning over a sexy young woman in a bikini. "How about one of Brownie's Heavenly?"

She holds a whole fish on a stick over a fire, and the bubble over his head contains a hot dog on a bun. They stand on a tiny island in the sea.

"Can't you cook anything..." was a frequent query from Dad to Mom and it wasn't said nicely. She boiled hot dogs in a cheap tin pot on the stove of our small kitchen, perfuming the air with the smell of hot fat. In the 1950s, we ate them with ketchup for lunch and sometimes dinner. She wasn't the greatest cook, but his harsh words never made things better. They made her cringe instead, and left us, their daughters, puzzled. Who was right, in this scenario? They both had reasons to belittle the other, and we were their captive witnesses.

We walked to and from school by ourselves, in those days, when little girls could safely move about alone. If you had to, you could pretty much walk all over our small town, and many people did. We all four had to, when Dad got laid off and couldn't afford the payments on our used black Chevy. When friends stopped to offer us a ride, Mom never said yes, mumbling after they'd passed that it was embarrassing to have to walk. It was a big relief to her and us when Dad went back to work and we could afford another used car.

In 1954, Dad waited in the car in the parking lot outside St. Stan's Elementary School, a big smile on his face. "I'm taking you to Brownie's for hot dogs."

The hot dogs were plump and juicy, the rolls soft and buttery. We even liked the onions and ground beef sauce on top. This was a good time with Dad, so often an angry guy. He had what Mom called "a short fuse." At Brownie's, it was nice to see him happy. Maybe we could relax a little. Dad loved to eat, not good according to Mom, though she'd shovel her leftovers onto his plate.

He bit his nails and got frustrated. Then he yelled, mostly at Mom, but sometimes at Judy and me, for things like scraping our forks on the plate too noisily. It gave me an upset stomach I tried to ignore, never making the connection between the pain in my gut and my heart. Judy cried easily but I tried not to, because if I did it would mean he won somehow. I couldn't let him win but sometimes it was impossible to keep the tears from falling. There was no comfort then, only angry looks from both parents – at us, at each other, at the world, it seemed.

At Brownie's, Dad talked not about our school days but about the hot dogs. "Do you want ketchup or mustard? Toasted bun? Everything on it?" He looked around to see if the other people noticed him there with us, his daughters. It felt to me like he was proud of us in public. Not like at home. I relaxed in the booth, watching the smiling folks who knew my dad only here, outside our house.

Most of them worked in the factory, maybe all through the night. There were three different eight-hour shifts, and sometimes my dad worked the one that started in the late afternoon. He didn't get home until we were in bed, and on those days we must have eaten dinner without him.

Dinner with him at home coud be tricky. Mom didn't like that he was fat and let us know he was thin when she met him. He spotted her across the mill floor and asked her for a date. I've seen the pictures of them back then. She had curly dark hair, and dark brown eyes. He looked like Bing Crosby, people said, and he liked to sing. Sometimes he sang at home, in Polish even, hymns and Christmas carols, or along with the radio. I don't think I ever heard him sing a whole song, not all the way through.

People who just met Dad said he was a nice guy. Maybe he was, at times, but it took a long time for me to believe that. It took growing up and seeing how complex humans are, to see and hear myself yelling at my husband and kids. To not want anyone to see or hear, to feel a pain in my heart at the sight of their sad faces. To know where I learned to be this way.

A hot dog can make me smile or cry, depending.

ORCHID IN THE SNOW

We all want to believe we are loved, and we will find the evidence for it in even the coldest of places.

In childhood memories of my hometown, winters are long, cold and bleak. I moved away after college, and you could not pay me enough to live there again. My father, though, was used to the cold. In my mind's eye, he stands husky, bundled in a heavy coat, hat and gloves, leaning on his snow shovel.

Pushing snow around was a regular part of winter in Amsterdam, New York, as sure as swatting black flies when the sweet air of summer rolled in. In fact, pushing anything around, including my mother and, to a lesser extent my sister Judy and me, suited my father just fine.

My shoulders involuntarily rose toward my ears whenever he was around, even as a fifty-year-old woman, and yes, even today, remembering.

What little I know of his demons – an alcoholic dad who beat him, a cold and distant mother – is a weak explanation and a poor excuse for the way he behaved toward those he loved. In my father's house, before the age of six, I learned words I was not to say, words that brought my mother to tears, bellowed words that blew through our house with no warning, and no place to hide. When I was old enough, I biked to the woods at the end of our street, to the safety and peace of a glade of oak trees.

But when winter arrived, there was no place to go. There was only the little white house where my father's rage could erupt at any time. Outside, snow built up in great white mounds even before the plow went down our street and before the last flake hit the sidewalk, my father was outside, doing a man's job. With a wide metal shovel and the strength of his arms and back, he scraped the sidewalk and the driveway clean. No snow blower then, nor did we have a garage, and for a year or two, no car. My parents worked in the mills where layoffs meant no paycheck and unemployment benefits would not cover both the mortgage and car payments.

My father, frustrated by a life that was not what he expected, berated Judy and me for making noise with our forks at the dinner table. He scolded me for hitting the wrong keys while practicing the piano. He demanded to know why my report card had a B instead of all A's. I longed for a father like my friends Franny and Christine had, the kind who held you when you cried. Sometimes I stood in their houses and watched, mesmerized by the sight of love.

Yet now and then, he was different. A hot summer night of shouts and tears, he stalked out the door, came back with four ice cream cones already melting over his hands. Cold sweetness traveled past the lump in my throat. One Sunday afternoon my mother, sister and I visited him at work, where he was a lone security guard in a cavernous warehouse. Eleven and fourteen, we modeled our new plaid coats and matching clip on hats, puzzled by his tears as he smiled and nodded, wordless.

Years passed until the night of the Christmas Ball. It was December 1963, and the snow was mythically heavy. Neither my boyfriend Marty nor I was old enough to drive and so as darkness fell, my father took the wheel of our used Chevy sedan and drove us to the Ball in a blizzard.

I held my satin pumps above the drifts and climbed into the back seat, the hem of my turquoise secondhand cocktail dress hanging below my coat. Marty held the door for me then followed me in, his shiny black shoes wet with melting snow. My wrist corsage, a baby orchid, lay nestled inside a clear plastic box on his lap.

A few weeks before, an assassin had killed the president, and was killed himself, the following Sunday, on live TV. We were still in a state of shock and uncertainty that would last the rest of our senior year. We needed to know that grownups were in charge. In living rooms, in classrooms, and on street corners, our parents and teachers wondered if a dance was still appropriate. Finally, our principal consulted the school board. Yes, they decided, the Christmas Ball could go on as planned.

Now giant flakes of snow blew against the windshield of my father's car. Marty and I stared ahead, the orchid trembling in its box. My father's breath puffed out in little clouds as he cleaned off the snow with a long handled brush and climbed into the driver's seat. More snow melted on the shoulders of his jacket. Underneath his wool cap, his ears were red as he started the engine and pressed the gas pedal. The car slid a few feet to the left then right, before his gloved hands steadied the wheel and we moved down Catherine Street at a quiet crunching crawl.

Inside the car, hot air blowing at our feet made the only sound. Snow covered the windshield as fast as the wipers cleared it off. "Damn snow," my father said, toning it down for the boy whose ethnicity he would insult when he dumped me in the spring. We didn't know that yet. Nor did we know about the years of turmoil our country was about to endure.

Marty bit his lip nervously, but I had seen my father's eyes in the rearview mirror, staring down the storm on my behalf. It mattered not a bit, that brief moment in time, what happened next nor what had come before. I had seen my father's hands on the wheel.

MATTERS OF FACT

Aunt Geneva said the baby died on the kitchen table. Bluntly, as was her way, she handed me a morsel of family lore. I had come begging for stories that summer afternoon. In town visiting relatives, I called her at her high-rise apartment, the last one she'd occupy.

"Come visit me," she said, her voice shrill and urgent. "And don't tell your mother!"

My mother had long ago told me that Stacia, the child who died, was fifteen months old. She called her "my little sister," though Stacia was born first.

Mom taught me to pump water for the flowers she planted on Stacia's grave, centering the tin watering can beneath the spout of an old metal pump beside the cinder-paved path around the cemetery. When I grew tall enough, I worked the long heavy handle up and down until water gushed into the can. All this for the flowers on the grave of a baby who died on the kitchen table before her sisters were born. It was the flu, my mother said, and I practiced a soberly sad nod like my mother's.

There would be three more girls after Stacia: Irene, Lucille, and Geneva. Each one of them loved to tell stories, frequently different versions of the same tale, but only Geneva laughed and cried often, embarrassing her sisters. She told me "secrets" I already knew because she or my mother had told me before: her father was adopted, her husband was divorced before he married her, she filled her baby brother's bottle with creek water.

Geneva was the "slow" aunt and talked with a rough ungrammatical speech, often punctuated by a nervous chuckle, but she wasn't uneducated. All but one in the family of six made it to high school during the Great Depression before leaving the classroom to help support the family. Mom said her tenth-grade teacher begged her mother to let her stay, and even help her in the classroom but Grandma said no.

Mom and her brothers worked in our city's carpet mills and Geneva was hired as a "domestic." Only Irene, crippled by polio, was allowed to stay in school and go on to train as a hospital lab technician. She proudly wore the mantle of most well-spoken, correcting her sisters' grammar whenever she saw the need.

Geneva, whom Irene called Genevieve, laughed the most and cried the easiest, which also embarrassed her sisters. "I'm a waterworks," Geneva said, blowing her nose into a hanky at their brother's funeral. Her sisters wept silently and at appropriate times, most often alone.

Irene said she cried in the hall outside her husband's hospital room where he lay dying of cancer. My mother cried alone when her father died, though I was in the house. After her brother delivered the news, she went into her bedroom and shut the door, leaving me alone in the living room to hear her muffled sobs. Though I was fourteen, it never occurred to me to go in and comfort her.

It never entered my mind, because, you see, I am one of these women, a generation younger. I envy friends who cry openly – at the movies, at funerals, at weddings, in sorrow and in joy. Tears burn my eyelids and fill my throat, but I hold them in. When I see someone cry, I wish I could do the same, but I don't know how. I tell sad stories like the sisters in a matter-of-fact way although tears well in the eyes of my friends. There is a secret satisfaction in this: others break down while I remain strong. The emotions are there just beneath the surface, pricking at my throat, my eyelids. I just can't let them show.

Perhaps the three sisters in my family believed their pain was too great to share, and best borne alone, in hiding. Perhaps they believed they could keep it small by doing so, that showing their sorrow would somehow enlarge it until it became truly unbearable. I don't know.

I know how to cry: in my room, in the car, in the shower. I can put my hand on a weeping friend's shoulder or hug my son when he is sad. It's only me, my mother's daughter, whom I don't know how to comfort.

THE HARTWICK COLLEGE MAN

A long time ago, in a land far away, an eight-year-old girl that was me stood alone in the Hartwick College parking lot. She was stiff, and scared and not sure what to do. My little family – mom, dad and sister – had just driven over an hour from home to Oneonta, New York. It was my first piano competition, and none of us knew what to expect. All of us were anxious. My parents, because of their tough childhoods in the Depression, believed in being tough, stoic, not showing fear. My sister and I tried, but we weren't quite as good at it as Mom and Dad.

Worst of all, I was here to be judged. Mrs. Winslow, my piano teacher, thought I was good enough for this competition and I did like to play, even composing my own little melodies. But this was more serious. Who would I be up against? Would strangers – everyone was a stranger here – be cold to me? Would I embarrass myself and my family?

A man in a tan windbreaker greeted my parents, so was obviously someone they knew. Then he walked over and bent down to my eye level.

"You go in there, Linda, and knock 'em dead!"

And just like that, I knew it could happen. I knew it was possible for me to perform well, even very well. My parents were not the kind to praise or comfort their kids. It was not how they were raised. They had problems of their own and didn't have much emotional energy for me or my sister.

This was unusual for me: having someone in my corner, cheering me on. In fact, it was so unusual I believed him.

Inside the building, I sat down at the piano, arranged my little fingers above the keys, and played a classical piece I've long forgotten. I won a blue ribbon.

I no longer play the piano, but I have never forgotten that man's kindness, and how he opened a whole new world of possibilities for the eight-year-old me. He never knew.

Yesterday, a young man sat on a bench beside our walking trail, head hanging, hands between his knees. I said "Hi" as I passed, then "Did you see the heron?"

"No, is there one?" he perked up.

"I didn't see it today, but there's one that hangs out here, around that little bend in the creek."

"I'll keep my eyes peeled."

Maybe he felt a little less alone, like the older lady really saw him. Maybe expecting a heron took him away from whatever made him hang his head.

I'll never know. The parking lot man never knew either. If I could have, I would have told him.

HOW CAN I KEEP FROM WALKING

In the Mohawk Valley where I grew up, sidewalks mapped my world. In the 1950s, in Amsterdam, New York, Kelly's Lumberyard, fragrant with freshly cut two by fours, scented my afternoon walk from school to home. Walking, always walking up and down the hills of Amsterdam. From our little white house on Catherine Street, I walked east to the corner of Lenox, then south two blocks to Partyka's Market on Crane Street for Camels for my father, Lady Betty bread and pimento loaf for summer lunch sandwiches. I walked west to the corner at Church, then three quarters of a mile downhill to St. Stanislaus Church on Cornell overlooking the mighty Mohawk, its waters sparkling in the sunlight or choking on blocks of winter ice. I walked three blocks south to the corner of Vrooman where

Franny Benosky, a short girl with bobbed brown hair and glasses waited, books in her arms, then another two blocks to Edson to meet Christine Skowronek, tall and blond. We three walked south again down Vrooman Avenue to Carolann Zrodowski's corner at the lumberyard, and west to Jay Street where the last in our group, Rita Konieczny lived. All of us trooped downhill on Church past the mills already half empty. Mohawk Carpet Mills had closed down just a few years before, and the buildings were now a hodgepodge of companies producing swimming pools, fiberglass, basketballs, and men's uniforms. My mother still worked there, and we would too, in the summers through high school and college. We walked to work there, too.

I walked to the corner mailbox at Church and Catherine to mail letters to boyfriends in college, my cousin in the Army in Vietnam, birthday cards to friends and relatives. The mailman walked down our street at noon every day but Sunday, his big leather bag over his shoulder, his face and arms tanned year-round.

Walking then was not a sport. We mowed lawns and gardened and played basketball or softball or tennis. We walked to get somewhere. But in the Sixties, almost every family owned a car (just one), including mine, and walking was for people who couldn't afford to drive.

Then hard times hit my family. My parents were laid off from their factory jobs, and Mom said we couldn't afford to keep our car. Dad always let her explain things like this, and when we walked to church - Mom, my sister and I – he went to an earlier mass. Mom was embarrassed when a friend pulled up alongside us and offered us a ride. She said no, thank you, we'd rather walk, it was a nice day, but we all knew she only said that to save face.

No one really preferred to walk back then, but that is what I long for now. I live in the country, on a 45-mile-an-hour state road with no shoulders. Veer out of your lane and your wheels are in the ditch, the drop off too steep to drive out of, and you are stuck, needing a tow.

I drive to town for groceries, dental appointments and all the errands of daily life, but I always leave time for a walk. About ten years ago, our township built a park on former farmland next to a huge development with thousands of homes and townhouses. It's on the way to town, and has a walking trail. Now that my sons have left home, and both my husband and I are retired from full time jobs, I long to start walking right outside my door. More and more, driving to a place where I can walk is a nuisance. Sometimes we drive to a county park with a manmade lake and paved trails, but on busy weekends so many speeding bikers pass, their call of "on your left" making me jump out of the way, it destroys the peace of the place for me.

You see, I find beauty in the walking as well as in the place. I love the way my body feels moving, my feet pressing down on the earth, comfortable shoes supporting me. My breath deepens in gratitude as I inhale the healing, clean air and the smells of the outdoors. Walking in town, the scents of car and truck engines, restaurant kitchens, and grass fill my nostrils. In the park, I inhale the moist fragrance of the pond with its ducks and turtles, the meadow grasses left unmowed to attract herons and water birds.

Sometimes while walking I listen to a Patty Griffin album or the recorded chants of Mohawk women or Hildegarde of Bingen. On some days, I mentally work out problems as I walk, or plan the rest of my day. But often, my walks become a meditation. I breathe and step consciously, watching the earth, the grass, the birds, the houses, the people and their dogs. As I observe and move along, awareness grows that I, too, am a part of it all.

So has it come full circle for me, all this walking? When I was young, I walked to get to school, church, work, my friends, to my grandmother's house. I walked a mile downtown for a lipstick at Holzheimer's department store or a Coke at Rapello's Drugs. Always on a mission, the end was the reason for the trip's beginning. Now, my walking is my exercise, my destination the beginning, the place I started.

As I walk in meditation, hymns sometimes come to mind, perhaps because the only time I sing these days is in church. I remember the line from the Shaker hymn, Simple Gifts: "'tis a gift to come round where we ought to be." As I walk consciously, stepping forward in awareness as my life proceeds to its final destination, I come round to where I ought to be, and find it is where I have been all along. I have come to the here and the now. The gift of aging is that now, when I am walking, I know it.

REID HILL MEMORIES

In my dreams of Reid Hill, I am walking, always walking.

My parents built a new home on Catherine Street in 1950, three blocks north from my maternal grandparents' second floor cold water flat on James Street. Grandma didn't get hot water from a faucet until many years later. My mom, little sister and I walked from Catherine down Lenox, right on Crane, then left on Vrooman to Edson Street, where we turned right at the public school we Catholic kids never attended, and finally arrived at the top of James Street where Grandma and Grandpa lived at number 9.

We entered the enclosed back porch and climb the musty smelling dark stairway up to Grandma's kitchen door. We always entered at the back and exited at the front. After a visit which included potato chips or pretzels and an ice cold Coke, Grandma took us to the top of the front stairs and down we'd go, slipping our hands along the ornate oak banister all the way to the open front porch, then down more wooden stairs to the street. I think I could probably do that walk blindfolded all these many years later, so imprinted in my brain was the route and the enticing anticipation of safety and love at the end.

After graduating from St. Stanislaus Elementary School on Cornell Street, my friends and I went to the public junior high. High school tuition at St. Mary's was too steep for our millworker parents. It was the fall of 1960. John Kennedy was running for President and we were very excited at the prospect of a fellow Catholic winning the White House for the first time. Just about everyone we knew was a Catholic and a Democrat. We were 14 years old. Our fathers had fought in The War and come home safe. Our small world was a free and exciting place where the sun was always shining.

Every weekday morning, I started the trek, my arms full of books. I rounded the corner on Lenox and turned right on Crane where Frannie Benosky waited. Together we walked down Vrooman to meet Carol Ann Zrodowski who came over from Mathias to meet us.

All three of us crossed over on Edward at the lumberyard and headed over to James Street to pick up Rita Konieczny, the last of our foursome. I loved walking past that lumberyard. The fence was too high for me to see inside but I could smell the fresh cut two by fours, a scent that even today means hope and promise and newness.

My girlfriends and I walked down the Jay Street hill to Theodore Roosevelt Junior High on West Main Street. The afternoon return trip was pretty much the same unless one or more of us had an after-school activity. Sometimes one of our fathers would give us a ride home.

It was only a year, and then we were off to Wilbur Lynch High School, a longer walk and new adventures on a different hill.

MRS. BROWN'S TEARS

I see her still, standing before our civics class, tall and slim in a tailored suit. In ninth grade, I thought she was very smart and often funny. When she strode down the halls of Theodore Roosevelt Junior High, her stacked heels made a loud noise on the wooden floor.

It was October 1960. John F. Kennedy was running for President of the United States. Our school had no computers, no air-conditioning, and no women wearing pants. I would not hear about women's liberation for years, but Mrs. Arlene Brown was about to teach me something about standing up for yourself.

On that sunny October morning, I was 14 years old. I never raised my hand or spoke in class. In church, I sat in the pew like a porcelain statue. I was especially afraid of doing or saying the wrong thing, so I did not move or speak.

Mrs. Brown's voice was always loud, but that day in her civics class, it shook and had a higher pitch. Tears shone in her large brown eyes.

"I am very angry today, because we are not going to the John F. Kennedy rally on Grove Street, as we planned." She stopped to take a breath. "Mr. Turner, our principal, feels we would appear to be endorsing Kennedy for President. I promised to take you to see Richard Nixon, too, if he comes to town, but Mr. Turner will not allow that either." She paused for another deep breath and I saw her hands shake. "I am sorry, because I wanted to take you to see American politics in action. And I am very, very angry at Mr. Turner. "

The class fell silent, shocked that she stood up to her boss. For me, however, it was much more. For the first time, I saw a strong woman cry angry tears, and my world opened up like a flower. My teacher refused to be an acquiescent female or to sugar coat the truth.

On that autumn day in 1960, Mrs. Brown didn't get what she wanted, and I have no idea how this affected her job, but sometimes good things grow from disappointment. Watching her, I found my voice.

It has never been easy for me to speak through tears, but when I do, I like to remember her, standing tall, filling my head with possibilities.

PINE LAKE

A summer Sunday afternoon in the 1950s: in the foothills of the Adirondack Mountains, Pine Lake waits for our black Chevy to pull into the parking lot. It watches as my parents, my sister and me pop the heavy doors and climb out with towels, picnic basket, folding chairs. Other cars bring aunts, uncles, cousins, grandparents.

The lake is always cold to us kids, and shallow for a long way out. It's easy to see the minnows, tiny pebbles and plants below the surface. We stir up the muck with our feet and build sand castles, hard-packed and molded in pails upended on the beach.

Fifty years later, the sharp scent of pine still clings to my soul. I cannot smell it without feeling cold wet sand between my toes. I need a white bread and bologna sandwich.

At Pine Lake, our mothers handed out wax-paper wrapped lunches. They passed a paper bag of fat plums from aunts to cousins to uncles to grandparents. The plums were yellow-green, warm, soft and juicy. I recall my father's voice: "Here, have a greengage." He loved to say the name over and over. "These are the greengage ones, from our backyard."

We kids sat on a wooden picnic bench, our bodies in wet bathing suits, wrapped in thin striped beach towels. There were six of us and the food we shared was more delicious than the same things served at home.

Our grandparents passed the afternoon on wooden folding chairs in the shade. He was a small man in a white shirt with black arm garters, on his head, a straw hat with a black band. And she, white-haired and smiling, wore a pastel housedress, thick brown stockings and laced tan shoes. Grandpa liked to walk off by himself to look at a tree or pick up a pinecone and show it to one of the grandchildren. From time to time, Grandma handed out the food she'd brought: bags of potato chips, bunches of ripe yellow bananas.

^^^

Today on a walk in the park, I caught the scent of pine again. And when those afternoons came back to me, so clear in every detail, I saw one thing I had forgotten: In all those years of Sundays at the lake I could not swim.

In a snapshot taken there, I stand at water level, my arms stretched wide in a phony side stroke, my bathing suit above the water. The white rubber cap on my head will never get wet.

My mother learned to swim at the Y before I was born and did laps there with my aunt. Afterward, she said wistfully, they showered and talked with other women in the locker room as they dressed. But no more. At Pine Lake, with me, she waded only to her waist.

My father swam parallel to the beach with slow even strokes. My sister and cousins splashed around with me but I don't remember any of them swimming.

In the snapshot, I am posed, faking it. My mother said I looked like Esther Williams, the Olympic swimmer and movie star, but even then I knew it wasn't true. I felt phony, all costume and no real identity. And I thought that was okay. I treasured the photo, squinting at it, picturing Esther, then me, Esther, then me. Did I really look like her? Could I become her someday?

My parents took care of me, fed me, kept me safe and warm, and bought me the ruffled bathing suit and rubber cap. But now they're gone, and I have a question I can't ask them: Why didn't they teach me to swim?

One Sunday, my Uncle Lenny swam all the way across Pine Lake. Grandma and Grandpa watched him from the edges of their chairs. Without a word, he walked slowly into the water, then dove and swam away.

"Matka Boska!" Grandma whispered, a Polish prayer. "Mother of God!" She kept her eyes on the retreating figure of her forty-year-old bachelor son. We kids stopped playing and watched the dark sphere of his head as it bobbed away from us, his arms breaking the water, the left, the right... They stopped. We couldn't see him. A breathless moment and... our eyes squinting in the sun, we spotted him climbing onto a rock on the opposite shore.

"Is it him?"

"Did he make it?"

"Is that Uncle Lenny?" The lone figure sat on the rock and raised one arm.

"He's waving!"

"It's Uncle Lenny!"

"How will he get back?" We stared across the lake until

a few minutes later he dove again, returning with the same unhurried crawl.

Another lake: Sacandaga Reservoir, 1960. My friend, Vivian, drives her own motorboat. I'm at her birthday party and we decide to go out on the lake. Vivian's father must take the wheel because one of us girls, he said, could not swim. We'd be safer this way. He smiles and looks ahead at the water. Every one of the five girls in the boat knows the non-swimmer is me. It's my fault Vivian can't take us out alone to speed across the sparkling waves. My parents and cousins are not here for me. There is only Vivian, her dad and her swimming girlfriends. Embarrassed, I say nothing.

A decade later: a sailing weekend on Lake Hiawatha. Friends leave me sitting on the dock. "We're just learning to sail and we always capsize; we can't watch out for you if you can't swim." Embarrassed again, I smile gamely, and say nothing. But times have changed. It's the 1970s and women everywhere are raising my consciousness. I cannot avoid it. As I watch from shore, I have an exciting thought: This time, I can do something for myself.

The next day, I sign up for swimming lessons. With a few instructions, and a little practice, I learn to let go of the side of the pool. Each lesson, I use my legs and arms to power my body farther through the water. After eight weeks of classes, a neighbor sees me at the town pool and says, "You swim like a fish!" I can't believe it. Not me... Not like a fish. But maybe...like myself.

As life goes on, I swim in other pools, lakes and the ocean, loving the water, loving the movement as my arms part it, gliding through. I swim until I dare to believe I do it well. And like my uncle on that summer afternoon, I slowly and steadily swim away from the posed little girl in the picture, the one who is faking it. I swim not knowing where I'll go, trusting I will stay afloat, working with the water to support me.

I learn that astrologically, I am a Water Sign and that according to ancient philosophers, water is the mother of all things. I am pleased to find that in water, I am at home.

In my larger life, as if swimming there, too, I move away from the girl and toward the woman I become. She speaks for herself, looks for what she needs, and asks the stored-up questions.

When a summer breeze takes me back to Pine Lake, my uncle is there, sunlight glinting on the water as he waves to me from the distant shore.

MY GRANDFATHER'S EAR

I hold in my hand a shell, brown and white. It curves inward; light purple colors the shadow inside, like the dark depths of my grandfather's ear. I long to crawl inside it.

I want to know him again and for the first time. Who was he, what were his innermost thoughts behind that shell-like ear I remember?

I believe I could get to him, his essence, through his ear. At the end, he lost his hearing. The details of his final illness are vague to me now; I was only fourteen. I knew he was ill. He was seventy-four. Standing together in the middle room of the second-floor flat he shared with my grandmother and their son, my uncle, I was almost as tall as he was.

"I can't hear you anymore," he said, waving a hand toward the side of his head. Did I comfort him? Probably not. By then, I was already practiced in the stiff upper lip, never "breaking down" if I could avoid it. I may have said, "It's all right." I felt his love in his grieving.

We weren't alone in the room. There was always someone else, my mother, grandmother, sister, uncle. My mother, trying to cheer him, told me to show Grandpa my nails. I had polished them in the popular color for eyeshadow and nails that year. "Blue!" he said and smiled. But then we were silent again, not having the words.

My grandfather was a small, quiet man, a peaceful presence in the life of my extended family. When I was a child, he was often in our house, taking care of me and my sister while our parents worked. One day, she and I got into a fight over something I've long since forgotten. We ran around the house, yelling and crying. Grandpa was at least as upset as we were. He followed us from room to room, pleading, "Stop," "Don't cry," "She didn't mean it."

My grandfather's ear was well-trained in Russian. He learned the language as a boy growing up in Poland. Which words did he learn first, the Polish or the Russian? I wish I knew more. Polish at home, I think, and Russian at school.

Once he read to me from the New York Daily News. In a page one picture, people carried signs printed in Russian. It was during the Cold War, 1960. Americans were interested in what was going on in Russia, but I'll never know what it was that day. Grandpa was pleased, I know that. He pointed to the signs and carefully pronounced the Russian words for me. If I sat here forever, I would still not remember what they were, or the sound of his voice reading them to me. I wasn't interested, then. Fourteen, and head of my class, I didn't need to know any of the things he tried to teach me. The Old Country stuff was for old people like him, and though I loved him, it was a patronizing kind of love for an old man whose time had come and gone.

At the end of a typical day at St. Stanislaus School, I walked into the little club where Grandpa tended bar. Dark wood, sparkling bottles and a big mirror behind him, he reached under the bar and brought out a Hershey chocolate bar. He took me as a toddler on his lap, and showed me liquor ads in men's magazines like Esquire, teaching me to recognize Old Crow, Four Roses and others.

My grandfather's ear was small, like him, and always open for me, like his face. A half-wreath of black hair encircled the back and sides of his otherwise bald head. Even at the end, his hair never turned gray.

My mother told me a story that happened when she was a child. Grandpa worked in a butcher shop and one day, a man walked in the door with a young lamb in a sack. He asked Grandpa to butcher the lamb. Grandpa didn't like the idea, but he agreed. Alone in the shop, he cautiously peered into the sack. The lamb looked up at him. After a bit of time, he gathered the courage to put the sack on a table. He then removed the lamb from the sack, took out his knife and quickly cut the throat of the lamb, but not before the lamb looked at him again and baaed.

Grandpa later told me himself that it was a true story and that the lamb was crying "Mama." He told the man to never again bring a live animal to the store.

I saw him smile, I saw him cry, but I never saw him angry. With him, I felt safe. I wish I could feel that way again.

My grandfather's ear was clear, translucent so that light came through the outer shell and lit the tiny black hairs inside.

Now that I am sixty, I have time. Done with school and career, my days are my own creation to do with as I wish. And what I do now is sit and look at this little brown-and-white shell in my hand, turning it over.

What I am now is a woman frustrated by my inability to know the only man who loved me without condition, who died the year I was fourteen, long before I realized that who I was might have something to do with him.

LIFESAVER

I almost died in Partyka's Market, right in front of the meat counter, but I don't remember that. I heard the story in my mother's words, deep inside a trauma-free part of me that still echoes there, a lifetime later.

Outside, sweet pea vines climbed white strings toward the sky in a garden lush with snapdragons, zinnias, peonies, and hollyhocks. My father often sent me there for a pack of Lucky Strikes, and the grocers, brothers named Bill and Ray, made me promise they were not for me. Sometimes it was a loaf of white Lady Betty bread I was there for, always slowing my steps beside the garden, enchanted by its messy wildness.

. . .

The grocers' sister lived above the store. As a little girl, I was fascinated by her, leaning out the upstairs porch, pegging clothes to a line that stretched across the yard and down to a cinder block shed. Sometimes she was down in the garden, smiling shyly among the summer blossoms. She never spoke. When my mother was with me, she told me not to stare, because the sister was simple. I never knew her name, but I would say, even then, she looked safe and happy.

Inside the market, Bill and Ray smiled down at me from behind the counter. I stared into a glass-cased display of pimento loaf, bologna, and the liverwurst I still love. They teased me about my Luckies and gave me a free slice of bologna. We called it "baloney" before I knew how to spell it. I felt safe inside their little store, blocks from home, where my father could start yelling at any moment. A dropped spoon, spilled milk, or noisy piano practice could bring on a tirade and where would I hide? Down at the corner store, nobody yelled, ever.

Until I left home for college, that little corner market was a touchstone of my familiars. I passed it on the way to grade school and met my friend Franny on that corner. Sometimes on Saturdays we took the bus "downstreet" to department stores.

I must have been about four the day I stood with my mother in front of the meat counter, sucking on a Lifesaver candy. Suddenly, I choked and wheezed and struggled for air. Before my mother could move, a traveling salesman grabbed both my ankles in one hand, turned me upside down and clapped me sharply on the back. The Lifesaver popped out onto the hardwood floor, she said, but I only remember her telling of it.

I drove past Partyka's Market the other day. The windows were covered in cardboard. The garden is a plot of grass. Bill and Ray are gone. Maybe, like me, they didn't remember that choking incident. I bet the salesman did. I hope that, as the world grew more complicated, he recalled, like me, the simple kindness inside those walls and the glory of color behind them.

PART II

CONNECTIONS

OCTOBER DANCE

I thought about dancing this afternoon. Outside my window, orange maple leaves cling to branches and dance in the sunlight, holding on for just a little longer: a week or two or maybe only days. The leaves and I don't know for sure. Still we dance.

Clear sunlight touches the very top of the tree. It glints on the upstairs windows of a row of townhomes across the street, not with the hot glare of summer, but the warm glow of a fading Pennsylvania season. Winter's gray luster waits in the wings.

Beneath the maple, my stone Buddha sits on soft brown earth, his lap covered with red orange leaves. Above his head, the branches move again, dancing the leaves in a gust of wind. They shake in a sudden flurry then settle to rest as I think of my friend Patti.

She wrote in today's email about teaching her grown daughter to make her famous Swedish tea ring, about having tea with friends after they play on her private paddle board court, about her grandson stacking wood on the porch. She is dying. Her last chemo treatments may hold it off but each day is precious now. She shares her messages with a long list of friends. "You can find the good in everything," she writes. "I no longer worry about eating that extra piece of cake."

The other day I watched a Youtube video of a young doctor dancing before her double mastectomy. The only one in the room not wearing a mask, she pranced around the operating room with her surgical team, her eyes and body suffused with joy.

As the calendar year draws closer to its end, the coming holidays bring joyful anticipation to children, happy memories to grownups, and for some of us, a hint of finality. For a few weeks I woke up crying, my thoughts on what had been and could be lost.

Yesterday, I went to lunch with three longtime friends. Each woman took her turn in the dance of words around the table, telling of a painful knee, an unhealthy grandchild, a stressful job, a son's blindness. I felt the other people we brought to the table in our stories. I felt their dances, too, mingling and touching and drawing still more people in until I sensed the pattern of all our connections though I could not see it with my little eyes. I know I am lucky; I know we create our own happiness, in spite of everything.

At my high school reunion, my friend was talking at another table and her husband didn't want to interrupt her when his favorite number came up on the DJ's play list. I heard myself say, "I'll dance with you," not knowing what that might entail. He gave me a skeptical look, took my hand and cautiously led me into a familiar kind of jitterbug swing as I leaned back into his hand and let him push or pull me around the dance floor. The concentration required to pay attention to the music, my feet and the directions of his arms all at the same time was exhausting, exhilarating and just plain fun. "You're a good follower," he said, and this time I knew it was a compliment.

I don't often get a chance like that. My husband doesn't like to dance, though he gamely tries at weddings, to humor me. Twice a week, I plan my day so I can hit the gym at 11 for zumba class where I dance to Latin rhythms, oldies rock and roll, and even the rap I would never listen to otherwise. Women of all sizes, shapes and ages, glide and sway and turn while our vivacious young instructor encourages us to shimmy and "shake what ya got." We can't help but laugh and believe that we can.

The seasons will come and they will go, and they will come around again. Some of us will be here still, while others will pass on and new faces take their place. We can grieve. We can regret. We can fight what we can't control. Or we can learn to dance.

LOVE, FORGIVENESS, FOOTBALL

When I watched the Eagles with my husband, I learned by asking. What was that penalty for? Why wasn't that a touchdown? How many legs have to be in the end zone? How long does he have to hold the football before he can drop it?

I would never have asked my father any of these questions. I was afraid of him. He loved me, I know, but sadly, didn't know how to connect with me as a person; a girl, a woman. A daughter. He couldn't teach me about football, or men, or driving a car, or anything, really. It would have been too fraught for both of us. My dad had a temper. Big time. He yelled at my mom, cursing her, and criticizing my little sister and me for minor infractions like mistakes on the piano, or making too much noise with our forks. What an unhappy man he must have been.

He died twenty years ago, long enough for good memories to return. The first time my husband and I went to a Trenton Thunder game, my dad was there in my head, his happy voice cheering all the way from his big easy chair in front of our TV in Amsterdam, New York. I remembered sports announcers calling out names and words from long ago. Roger Maris. Mickey Mantle. Bunt. Fly ball. Bullpen.

In football season, it was Joe Namath who turned our tiny living room into a happy place. Handoff, huddle, line of scrimmage. I hear the words, I hear my dad happy, I feel safe. Later, he might sling an insult at my mother. Stupid ass. For crying out loud. You don't know nothin'. And she would cry or say something back.

I learned my snotty replies from her, I guess. My anger came out at my son and husband, and sometimes my friends, as if I carried it through the years from my father's house and finally, too heavy, let it spill out on the ones I loved, the ones who made a safe harbor for me.

But this is how I know he loved me. I saw him cry when I first walked in heels at fourteen, when he held my baby son, when we drove away from his house after Christmas. He brought us ice cream cones after one big fight, the melting treats dripping down his hands because he'd carried them for blocks. This is how I saw his love, his regret, his inability to say it any other way.

When he was an old man, I found the courage to say I loved him. You're a good girl, he'd reply, and I knew that was the best I would get. It was all right. I needed to say it. I feel sorry for the little boy I knew he was, beaten by his alcoholic father who died when my dad was only twelve, the things my mother told me out of earshot. He never grew up, she said, trying to explain.

As children, we take what we can get. I never sat and watched a game with him. I was too scared. But here I am, an elder woman, looking back at the goodness there.

My son has a temper too. He had a hard time with bullies in school, and sometimes scared me when he lost control, but now he seems content. When he started coming over on fall Sundays to watch the Eagles, I loved to see him so excited and happy. Now he watches at Chickie's and Pete's with friends, and we text during the game. I'm grateful for that.

So, this is about feeling connected to two men who scared me. And how the Eagles remind me of love and forgiveness. Wounded, even underdogs, we manage to rise again, to ask for what we need, to apologize without words. We hang in there. We survive.

YOU HAVE TO EAT LUNCH

The empty house echoes as I work. Here in my parents' postwar version of the American Dream, women's voices come back to me. Women who worked at home and in factories, raised me, my sister and my cousins, read McCall's and Good Housekeeping, and always had a fresh cake or a plate of cookies ready for whoever might drop in. They are the kind of women you can count on, the ones who show up unannounced before you even think of asking. Ceil is short and bouncing with energy, her face sprinkled with light brown freckles, her sandy hair cut short as if any other style would take too much time. She married my Uncle Edwin in Amsterdam, New York soon after World War II and poured her energy into her home and family. Ceil loved to sew and made beautiful smocked dresses for their daughter, Peggy, who now lives in Florida. She loved to dress up and go ballroom dancing with Uncle Ed at the Century Club, a white pillared building on Guy Park Avenue, the grandest street in town. One of five sisters, Ceil is often on the phone. I would not be surprised if she was the first person who signed up for "call waiting." "Just a minute," she says when I phone her, "My sister is on the other line." True to her word, she is back with me in a minute or less because her sisters all live in the same town and she talks to at least one of them every day, but I am calling "long distance." I remember her most at my parents' kitchen table, sitting before a creamy cup of coffee, her bright red lipstick print on the rim, a smoldering cigarette in a glass ashtray. She was the very picture of sophistication, frequently dropping the names of women's and children's stores–Gabay's, Holzheimer and Shaul, the Chatterbox–as if she went there every day. One afternoon when I was in high school, we ran into each other at Woolworth's. She bought me a Coke at the counter and asked about my life as if it was important. Like most girls, I needed that kind of validation. As I matured, I pushed back against my mother's example, but my aunts were a step apart. They carried no judgment or emotional baggage and I knew I could count on them to be my personal cheerleaders. Ceil worked in retail herself now and then, at a fabric store and a card-

and-gift shop but her real talent was homemaking. I treasure her handwritten recipes for banana bread, stuffed cabbage, and potato chip cookies. I may never use them, but they are sweet reminders of the long, slow days when women baked from scratch. When I was growing up in the Fifties, a great deal of time and effort went into so-called women's work, but as a young woman in the Seventies, I believed that time would have been better spent on careers outside the home. My mother and her friends worked in factories, and felt lucky simply to have jobs and to own their homes, but we, their daughters came of age during feminism's Second Wave. We had more opportunities than our mothers ever dreamed of. Still, we lost something when we denigrated the skills of homemakers. Hillary Clinton famously stated during her husband's Presidential campaign, "I suppose I could have stayed home and baked cookies" and her words became code for "strong women don't bake," though she never intended it that way. I'm sure she meant women should have many choices: homemaking, careers or both. But some of us, myself included, didn't want to talk about cookies at all. On the way to equal rights, we stepped right over the enjoyable parts of creating a comfortable home. Years after I baked a few cookies myself, I read an essay by Gloria Steinem. After many years working for women's rights, she noticed that her home had no personal touches. Her apartment was more like an office, filled with papers and books, basic furniture, and nothing personal. My Aunt Ceil never had that problem. Her home is full of knickknacks from her daughter's travels. She herself has been to Europe and up and down the East Coast and filled her home with found treasures. A sparkling glass bluebird perches on a windowsill. Hummel figurines are on display in a dust-free glass cabinet and beribboned blue towels invite my touch in the small bathroom. y other aunt, Willette, married Edwin's brother John. Descended from Irish immigrants, she taught herself to with my grandfather a Merry Christmas in Polish. Her once brown hair is pure white and her face opens in a wide smile. One afternoon, she gave me a ride home from high school. Feeling sick, I walked to her house, knowing she, like many women, would be home in the middle of the day. As she drove, she asked me about M bioStories 44 2012, Vol. 2 the upcoming prom and graduation, and like Ceil, made me feel she was really listening. Willette and John raised two sons who are now grown but still live with their families nearby. She worked for a while as a telephone operator and became the link between Mom's sister in California and the rest of the family in New York State. "Willette gets free long distance," my mother said, explaining why she never called her sister. Even when rates fell to a nickel a minute, our family still counted on Willette to relay news from the West Coast. One weekday afternoon when I was small, my mother and I dropped in on her, as people did back then, and found her praying the rosary. Mom apologized. "You'll have to start all over again." "Yes, I will," she answered cheerfully. Then she went to the kitchen, put out slices of homemade cake and poured coffee for Mom, a glass of milk for me. After I married and had children of my own, these impromptu visits were rare. Everyone was busy, it seemed, and lived far away from family. I became what Mom called a "career woman."

ow, on this early spring day, the sky is painted periwinkle blue, as only an Adirondack sky can be. Hundreds of tiny green leaves wave like flags on gnarled trees in the backyard of my mother's house. Inside, I clean out the last of her belongings. My father has been gone a year, and Mom is in a nursing home. Ceil and Willette held a garage sale on the sidewalk in front last week. On this day, I have driven north from my Pennsylvania home with my ten-year-old son to clean out what remains, the things no one will buy. Threadbare bath towels, a plastic clothes hamper, costume jewelry in a dirty pink box. Used dress patterns, spools of thread, dust rags. Two framed Easter cards on the wall. The empty house echoes as I work. My son's Game Boy chirps from the living room as I finger the worn remnants of my mother's hard life. I work alone, Mom's voice in my ear: "Linda's the independent one." Outside in the driveway, a car engine stops and doors slam. The back doorbell rings and before I can answer it, my mother's kitchen door swings open. The aunts walk in laughing, arms laden with brown paper bags. On the old Formica table, Ceil and Willette unpack lunchmeat wrapped in white butcher paper, small jars of mayonnaise and mustard, fresh tomatoes, and a package of rolls. "We knew you were here," they say, smiling. "You have to eat lunch."

A CONNECTING THREAD

In the thirty years after I left my mother's house, I never missed her. Yet it pleases me now, in my sixth decade, to find a connecting thread.

Mom was an excellent seamstress. She made her living at a sewing machine and came home to sew most of our clothes in the evening. She had decidedly mixed feelings, proud of her skill but trapped in a life of manual labor. I remember her frequent complaints—her thread broke, there was a mistake in the pattern, she couldn't find her scissors.

"Goldarn it!" she'd mutter.

Though she seemed to take little joy in it, she always produced a beautiful garment. The prom dress she made me had a white lace fitted bodice, apple green slim skirt, and thin shoulder straps. The other girls wore dresses from Holzheimer and Shaul, the local department store, and two of them showed up at the dance wearing identical models. Mine was an original, custom made for me.

"Why did you tell them it was homemade?" Mom scolded. "They'll think you can't afford a dress from Holzheimer's."

"But they liked it," I said. "No one else can get one anywhere." She hadn't thought of it this way, and I could see that she wasn't sure what to believe. Her philosophy was to work hard, not enjoy it and never take credit for what you've done.

My mother's fingers cracked and bled from long hours in the factory, feeding parts of men's work pants into industrial machines. For a few years, she worked on basketballs; I can't imagine how she did it. She welcomed the occasional layoffs, though we needed the money. I was with her one day when she left the unemployment office with a job offer.

"Goldarn it!" she muttered as she grabbed my hand and marched out the door.

At home, Mom sewed in the tiny bedroom she and Dad shared. Her old Singer machine stood at the front window, looking out on the street. She slid a small padded bench Into the two-foot space between her machine and the foot of the bed. In the weeks before every major holiday, she'd make new clothes for herself, my sister, Judy and me.

"Linda, come and try your dress on!"

Uh oh. Time for another endless fitting. Mom dropped the dress over my head. I tried not to move as she tucked here and folded there, pinned the darts and removed the pins and did it all again, shaking her head in frustration. A curvature of the spine made my left shoulder lower than the right, my left hip higher, eliminated my waistline and condemned every sewing project to countless alterations. I grew bored and impatient. Unable to resist squirming, I got stuck with a pin.

"Ow!"

"Goldarn it! I told you not to move!"

I tried not to wet the dress with my tears.

"Just go." Mom lifted the dress over my head and turned away. I barely glanced at the back of her head covered with short, dark curls. Both of us tried so hard and failed. She couldn't make the perfectly tailored dress. I couldn't be the perfectly quiet little girl. I turned the glass doorknob, pulled it toward me and ran out.

Where was the picture of a happy mother and daughter sewing together? I'd seen them in McCall's magazine, and on the poster in the fabric store window. I wanted to be the little girl in that picture. I wanted a different mother. Maybe Betsy McCall's mother, the one that came with my paper dolls. Betsy and her mother were always having fun.

At the time, I thought that both sewing and I were a huge pain in the neck. Mom tried to teach me, but I never got the hang of it. I suspect it felt too close to being her. I didn't want to be so harried, so trapped in a difficult job.

Years passed without my sewing more than a loose button. I had a career, two children and a husband, and a house in the country. We needed new window treatments, but the cost was so shocking, I decided to make them myself. And that is how, shopping for drapery fabric, I fell in love with a computerized sewing machine. It threaded itself, came with six presser feet, and remembered your monograms. It did everything but make coffee.

I wished that Mom could see it; other memories came flooding back. The smell of sizing from the aisles filled with colorful bolts of cloth. The filing cabinets filled with patterns in paper envelopes. The huge catalogs on tables with high stools to sit and browse from, turning the pages, dreaming up a new dress... I remembered her then, leading me through the store, and I knew I was not my mother. I would not become her by learning to sew. And I had found something we shared, something about her I wanted to keep.

When I sew, each sound, each item I touch, becomes a memory that connects me to her. The feel of the tissue paper pattern, the placement of the pins attaching it to fabric just the way I watched her do it. The chop, chop of the scissors taking me back to the kitchen table that was her cutting board. The soft whir of the machine as my foot presses down on the pedal. The way I focus on my work, snipping loose threads and letting them fall..

I love all my tools—the rotary cutter and mat, the spools and bobbins, the snips and scissors, my stash of fabrics. I have some things from Mom's old sewing cabinet—patterns in her size, bindings and trims, her paper cutter. I like to see them nestled among the notions I bought for myself. Because my mother was so skilled, I believe I, too, can be good at this, and I want to be.

When I'm sewing, I feel like I'm standing on her shoulders, as she stood on the shoulders of women who sewed through the ages, making clothes, making art, making memories. And if only by a thread, I finally feel connected to my mother.

BREAD ON THE GRASS

We don't throw away bread," my mother said. She took a few quick steps to the metal trashcan near the kitchen sink and fished out the crusts inside.

It might have been a Saturday with both of us home at lunchtime. I would have been small, maybe seven. She probably made me a bologna sandwich with mayonnaise and a slice of tomato on Lady Betty bread and poured me a glass of milk. Lady Betty smiled at me from the outside of the white plastic bread bag, her hair in a curly brown up do.

"Grandma says bread is like the Host," my mother said, holding my discarded crusts in her outstretched hand. She meant the communion wafer, transformed at

Sunday Mass into the body of Christ. Grandma was Mom's best friend and confidante, the one she turned to when life was hard and there were no easy answers. She had come to Amsterdam, New York at the turn of the twentieth century, and now lived in a second floor flat, with no telephone or hot running water, seeing no need for either. During the Great Depression, each of her six children, one by one, left school as soon as they were old enough to look for work. Nobody wasted so much as a crust of bread.

An old Polish proverb says, "A guest in the home is God in the home." Most of Grandma's guests were family, but as soon as anyone crossed her doorstep she scurried to the cupboard for cake, donuts, potato chips, any food she could offer. For this wife of a grocery clerk, store-bought food meant she had money.

She taught me to say *chleb*, the Polish word for bread, as she sliced a fresh loaf, giving it her full attention, making of the act a little ritual of gratitude. I never saw her toss away a single morsel.

As I chewed on my crust-less sandwich, my mother stood beside me wearing her homemade skirt and a white blouse. Beneath her curly brown hair, the look on her face was serious but kind.

"We can feed the birds," she said. We tore the crusts into little pieces and piled them on my empty plate. I imagined tiny beaks happily munching, thanks to Mom, Lady Betty and me. Mom turned the worn brass handle on the back porch door, pulled it open and solemnly handed me the plate. I carried it as reverently as I had seen the altar boys carry the golden paten of consecrated hosts on Sunday morning.

Then Mom and I threw handfuls of the torn bread out the porch window. I waited for little birds to fly into our yard and discover the feast, but none came and quickly bored, I went back inside. The next morning, when I looked out the window, the bread was gone. Shy birds, I thought, like me, but at least they won't go hungry.

After I grew up and married, I learned to bake bread from a cookbook. "All natural" was the way to go, in food as well as childbirth. There would be no store-bought bread in my home. That approach lasted a year or two, until I had a full time job and a long commute. Because it was so easy to buy a loaf at the supermarket, I declared bread baking a skill for hippies and earth mothers who did not work outside the home. We met friends for dinner at restaurants, everyone too busy to cook.

At home, my little boys left their sandwich crusts on their plates, just as their mother did long ago. You can guess what I told them.

"We don't throw away bread," I said. "We can feed the birds." I showed them how to tear the crusts into pieces and scatter them on the grass for our feathered guests. Sometimes they even stayed to watch the birds peck at it.

Now that our nest is empty, bread is a "high carb" item my husband and I have cut back on. We keep our whole-wheat loaf in the fridge, but it still goes stale. Nobody wants the ends, dented and misshapen in the plastic bag. Outside my window, five bird feeders hold sunflower seeds, split peanuts and calcium-rich suet for strong eggshells. I have a discount club membership at the birdseed store. But none of that feels quite so holy as the simple act of tossing breadcrumbs on the grass.

STREET STORIES

He's an old man sitting, one I can't forgive. A man so like my father it frightens me. Because he won't apologize, I don't want to "let it go."

First came a couple of years of him frowning at me across the street as he sat in a lawn chair in his driveway, garage door open behind him. Then four years of friendly chats, putting up with grumpiness, followed by the climactic episode of fear.

A different old man sits around the corner, in his own driveway, sober-faced. He nods when I walk past, and never speaks or smiles at me. He drives a shiny black pickup truck with a blue line flag decal on the back window, the flag denoting support for police. Since these flag decals popped up recently as police brutality became a news story, I'm suspicious of their intent. Why does protesting harassment of Blacks by police inspire a statement in favor of law enforcement? This man scares me too.

My neighbor talks to Jake, despite his crabbiness. I'm not sure why. Several others ignore him. He's had the police called on him at least twice that I know of. Once, for yelling at a woman whose dog scared his wife. Another for threatening to shoot a neighbor's ex. A friend of my husband's who knew him years ago said he shot a dog for barking. He's raising his second Pug in the last eight years, and I don't understand his love for these dogs after shooting someone else's. My friend Karen came to see me when I was sick, bringing food. She asked if she could bring her dog and walk him with me, but when she got out of her car, Jake yelled across the street, "do you live around here?"

"I'm visiting my friend."

"You better watch where you walk him!"

I wish I had told him off when she came inside and reported that encounter. Scared to, I guess.

He reminds me of my father. In his old age, he sat on his back porch for hours, staring. I think my dad was depressed. Otherwise why sit in a wooden folding chair, the seat repaired with a cloth tied around a broken slat, watching out the open window? Not even traffic to look at, like Jake.

He looked out on a quarter acre of grass he mowed himself, on the back of the neighbors' homes, on shrubs and lilac bushes he'd planted long ago. When I was small and my dad was still working in factories, my grandfather babysat me and my sister. He looked out that porch and saw the newly built NYS Thruway from our house, but soon other houses blocked that view. My dad couldn't see that far. My mom wanted him to read or take a walk or get a hobby. He was a fat man all my life. He read only the local paper and the New York Daily News, a tabloid that was a regular read for me as a little girl because it was in our house and I escaped that way.

I want to meditate, to sit still for a time, but it's hard for me to settle down. I don't understand my dad. I don't really want to write about him.

I don't understand my neighbor either. He collects information, watching. He reported to me that my son was smoking. He yelled at the guy next door and I have ignored him since, maybe 3 years now.

He used to tell me things when I walked past. He had a bad childhood, a bad mother, he changed his Jewish name to Jones, he was anti-Trump because of his cheating the building trades Jake worked in. Steve still talks to him, and that feels like he's not supporting me, but he's not the one who was scared.

These scary old men make me wonder if my father influenced my choices in boyfriends and husbands. They say a father does. My first boyfriend was warm and friendly, but most of the others were distant, though none were as verbally abusive as my father. He swore and cursed my mother almost every day, so loud it made all three women he lived with cry. We were never close to him. Even in my fifties, I was afraid to be alone with him. A man in the grocery store yelling at a clerk made my heart pound. The clerk winked at me, probably because she saw my fear.

I don't like these old men. Why write about them at all? Writing helps me figure myself out, my life, my choices. And it helps me figure out big issues like forgiveness. I know it's something to aspire to. My Catholic upbringing taught that I needed it, must ask for it. Maybe that I deserved to be yelled at? That I must forgive those who hurt me, as Jesus did.

Another old man lives next door. I have never seen him seated in his driveway. He is short and loud and his hearing aids don't work so he shouts. He complained today that one of the townhouse owners in our development had painted their deck black, against the rules for color choices, and when he wrote a letter of complaint, the head office said the deck was "in compliance."

"How does this affect you," I asked.

"Well, why have rules if you don't enforce them," he said.

"I'm sorry it bothers you."

"Oh, I don't care, I can't wait to get out of here."

If he leaves, I could get a worse neighbor. Or a better one. If Jake leaves across the street, same deal. At least I wouldn't have somebody staring at me and all my visitors in nice weather. One of the good things about winter is there are no driveway sitters.

THE DARNING EGG

On a cold winter morning, I dug a pair of socks I knitted years ago from the back of my sock drawer, admiring the purple, black and olive-green stripes. Even though they are oversized and not smoothly shaped, for I never perfected my sock knitting, they felt great inside my boots. As the day went on, I noticed a hole in the toe of first one sock, then the other, when I removed the boots and walked through the house shoeless, in stocking feet as is my habit. Put your shoes on, I hear my mother say, as I go upstairs to put on a new pair of hole-free socks, tossing the others onto the floor of my closet.

Her voice comes with admonitions. Not endearments, for that was not her way. My father's words were often harsh, critical, verbally abusive. He called her names.

She coped by acting tough, impervious to pain. And even when he turned on us, his daughters, she offered no comfort. He wouldn't ever hit you, she'd say, because his father had beaten him. He would never do that to you.

We grew up afraid of loud voices, of anger, of our own truth. Afraid of self-care and compassion, for that would be weak.

My holy socks lay in the dark on my closet floor for a couple of weeks, waiting for me to do something until, one morning, I sat on the bed, socks in hand, debating my choices. My husband watched, bemused at my dilemma. How long have you had them? Years? Oh, well, you got a lot of use out of them anyway.

Still I was reluctant to discard my hours of craft and labor so freely. I remembered how hard it was to make them, and that I'd stopped after a few pairs. It was awkward to wield four double-pointed needles, and frustrating getting the heel right. They always turned out too big, like a bulge at the back of my foot.

My mother taught me to knit, but never socks. She would not have had the patience. She was always in motion: cleaning, cooking, sewing. Few are the memories of her sitting and reading a magazine: McCalls, Family Circle, Good Housekeeping, always scouring the pages for recipes or dress patterns. Always with things to do. Like me, I've been told.

Reading, knitting, and sewing are relaxing but can easily become projects, a way to show I'm accomplishing, achieving, gaining approval. But from whom? Mom and Dad are long gone. I'm a woman in her seventies. Surely, I can relax now. Can't I?

At loose ends one Saturday morning, I thought, at least I can do this, this one little thing, and feel productive. I can mend the socks. I hand threaded a needle with black thread to match the variegated sock yarn, pleased it made my stitches invisible, blending in with dark purples and greens. Pleased to feel a quiet satisfaction in this old-fashioned chore. I turned the first sock inside out and tucked my fist into the toe. Like my mother's darning egg, I thought, recalling her doing this very thing. I still have her wooden egg with a handle, the one she used to teach me to darn. I took it down from a shelf and turned the second sock over it. With quick small stitches, the way she taught me, I mended the hole, ending with a knot and a snip of the thread. And I wondered how it was that in a little house so fraught with worry and care, its walls echoing my father's rage, a bit of peace and safety still clings to my being, my soul, my little girl self. And I wonder what else I can mend.

PART III

OTHERS

OLD WOMEN AND OTHER STRANGERS

The line was long and moving at the pace of a dead snail, which is to say not at all. I was hungry and tired, and the cafeteria was noisy and hot. From behind me came a loud exasperated sigh. I turned to see a chunky old woman in a pink sleeveless shift peering around me to see what was holding us up. We were halfway through a weeklong women writer's conference, and the lines had long since destroyed my patience, too, but I kept quiet, hoping to discourage her from voicing the complaint I expected. Her darting eyes fixed on the English muffin on my plate.

"You have to toast that! " She said with a heavy German accent, spitting her T's at me like pellets. "You can't eat it like that!"

Oh, brother. Or in this case, sister. I was tired of eating and sleeping and living with four hundred women, each with her own issues. I wanted their feedback on my writing, especially those whose work I admired. But did they have to share their opinions about everything? World affairs, the weather, the dorm rooms, and now, my breakfast? Did this woman not know she had crossed a line?

I took a deep, centering breath, leaned toward her and answered in my calmest tone. "I'll eat it any way I want."

She smiled, surprising me. "My husband always says, 'why do you stick your nose in where it doesn't belong?' But when I see something wrong, I have to say it!" Her final "t" sprayed the air an inch from my face before she chuckled and moved to another, shorter line.

Over-controlling, I thought. What was her story? The question occupied my mind until I found a seat at a nearby table, forgetting her as I caught up with friends.

When she turned up later that afternoon in the same writing workshop as I, my shoulders tightened. I watched her find a seat and waited for her to see me, to remark on another "something wrong." She didn't. And as we listened to the instructor, wrote and shared our brief exercises, I learned some of her story.

She was a Holocaust survivor. As a young girl, she had lived for years in a concentration camp. And today, in class, she couldn't concentrate because her daughter might lose her child in a custody hearing that very day.

This explained everything to me. Who wouldn't want to over-control after being held prisoner for years, her life in someone else's hands? How many times had the possibility of loss been forced upon her? And here it was again, her life as a grandmother potentially destroyed by a judge in another city. Why not try to change the things she could, if only a stranger's untoasted muffin?

But later in the day, I met more women like her. And I began to run out of sympathy. There were so many of them, complaining about the heat, the air conditioning, the stairs... I didn't want to put up with crotchety old ladies, whatever their stories. I longed to be with happy, healthy people.

And yet, every day for the rest of that week, the old woman magically appeared before me: in class, on the sidewalk, in the dorm. She walked with a shuffle, like she was still in line in the cafeteria or maybe those camps long ago. I couldn't look away.

Concentration camps stand empty in the Poland of my ancestors. In my grandfather's village, people killed their neighbors in a frenzy of mob hysteria, while others hid Jews in their basements.

When I visited Poland a few years ago, a tour guide said "we feel a phantom pain," like the ache of an amputated limb, after the loss of so many Polish Jews. Amputated, I thought, like the Native Americans whose gifts we will never know.

It's hard for me to look away when I see injustice. Maybe it's in my bones, my DNA. To truly accept my country, like the young man in Poland, I must accept the whole of who we are -- the shadow side, the ugly, the times we have forgotten to be good.

Long ago, my New York neighborhood of Polish immigrants was rooted in fear of those who were different. I could easily hide there, camouflaged by my light skin and rounded face. Recently, the town council voted to sell an abandoned school building to a Buddhist group which planned to open a health and spirituality center. Many people opposed the sale, and put up signs urging a vote against it, afraid the Buddhists would bring in people they might not like. People who were different. Happily, hope won out over fear, or maybe the town just needed the money more than they needed to feel comfortable. More than they needed control.

It's different near Philadelphia, where I live today. We have plenty of "others," some of them friendly and some as rude and obnoxious as people have always been. I can't blame their ethnicity for that, any more than I blame my grandfather for the sins of the villagers he left behind. I feel safe here, creating my own happiness.

I'm willing to bet that some of the Buddhists in my old hometown will be lovely people and others, like the old woman at the writing conference and a few of my relatives, will be quite annoying. It can be hard to stay calm when the world is so diverse and noisy. I do understand. Sometimes I feel like I'm standing inside an ever-changing kaleidoscope.

I don't know what happened to the "toast your muffin" lady or her grandchild that day, but I believe she was in my life for a reason. Maybe that reason was to share her story - and mine - with you.

May there always be room in this world for cranky old ladies. Just in case I ever need it.

WALK IN WELCOME

"Choose color!" the reception shouts, and I walk quickly to the wall of nail polish bottles behind her head. There must be dozens here, frosted and shellac-bright, in shades from white through pinks and reds and browns to black. I grab a bottle of pinkish natural color and follow the manicurist to her station.

This is my first time in the nail salon, and though I'm turning sixty, it will be my first manicure. I chose this salon out of more than a dozen like it near my home, all in little strip malls, all run by Vietnamese immigrants.

The shop is busy on this rainy Saturday afternoon, and the workers chatter loudly to each other in a foreign language. Foreign to me, that is. The very young woman filing my nails smiles at me and tells me I've chosen a nice polish color. "Pretty," she nods her head at the bottle near our hands.

She laughs and shoots some words I don't understand at the male manicurist at the next station. The workers who chatter and laugh here are all Asians. The women customers are all Caucasians. My friend doesn't like to come here.

"They don't speak English very well," she says.

"What language are you speaking?" I ask my manicurist.

"Vietnamese," she answers shyly and files industriously at the edges of my ragged nails. "Go out tonight?"

We have a little conversation about my upcoming evening, but it's difficult, and so we finally shrug and smile instead.

The other customers stare at a small TV set mounted high in the corner, or flip through People magazines. None of them talk to the workers. Uncomfortable, I try again.

"Do you live nearby?" I ask as the small young woman clips my cuticles with a tiny pair of scissors. A frown line appears between her brows. Without lifting her eyes from her work she names a small town a few miles away.

"Are there any good Vietnamese restaurants there?" I ask. "I love Vietnamese food."

She shakes her head and places my hand in a small glass bowl of sudsy water. My nails are being groomed, I'm paying for the service, yet I feel I should be doing more. More than the blonde suburban ladies around us who ignore the salon employees, who flip the pages of their magazines and pop their chewing gum.

After all, I am the grandchild of immigrants. My grandparents came here from Poland at the turn of the twentieth century. They spoke no English and waited for hours at a train station before someone took them to a house where they would live while working in a broom factory in the city that became my hometown. Their courage gave me the life I have today, a comfortable, secure and happy life. I don't work with my hands, and here I am, today, actually getting them pampered by an immigrant. Maybe that's what makes me squirm.

Over at the reception desk, a golden statue presides over fresh oranges and fat red candles in glass holders. Shiny red flags with gold embossing decorate the walls, but I'm the only one here who looks at these things.

I'm not like these other white ladies I want to say to the woman who is holding my hand. *I understand your struggle. I want you to succeed.* But I don't say anything.

"Wash hands," my manicurist says, gesturing to the sink at the back of the room. Conspicuous, I go and do as she says, but no one is looking at me. I only feel it, myself, as though a sign covers my forehead. "New here," it reads, "doesn't know what to do."

They probably can't afford to eat out, I chide myself. *The rest of their families more likely work in the Vietnamese restaurants than eat there.*

"Pay first," the woman says when I am back at our station. I fumble for the bills in my wallet, not ready, and nervously manage to over-tip her. She polishes my nails with swift precision, two coats in "Innocence" and then a clear top coat. She walks around to my chair, lifts my purse and leads me to the drying machines. I need her to show me how to place my hands under the dryer. She presses the button to start the blower.

"Have nice day," she says, waving. "Bye, bye!"

Wait, I want to say. *I care about your life here. I welcome you.*

"You, too," I say feebly. When the dryer stops I stand and walk to the door, where I read, backwards from the inside, the words "Walk In Welcome."

This was hard, but I'll be back. My shiny nailed hand

pushes the door open, and somewhere my Polish grandma smiles.

STOP KISSING ME

Last month, in St. Mark's Square, a bearded Australian kissed my cheek. Twice. I didn't like it. I'd been standing under the roof of the shopping area that surrounds the square on three sides, waiting for my friend. We were with a group tour, and she went to climb the tower while I shopped.

"So what's this all about," a male voice asked, pointing to the scene before us. His accent was obvious, and while we chatted about the basilica, the tower, the square, a smiling blond woman and a tall blond teenaged boy appeared on either side of me, magically. We talked for a while. They were Australian musicians traveling the world. He wanted a picture, and drew us to a live piano performance where we posed in front of the stage, his arm around me. He kissed my cheek and my friend Pat, who had arrived, took another picture and he kissed my cheek again. His beard bristled against my skin and I bristled inside.

Either he or his wife asked for my phone number and email address, and I gave it to them. They were being nice, friendly, and what was the harm? It felt a little intrusive, but so what? After we walked away, I told Pat he seemed aggressively friendly, and the kiss on the cheek felt intrusive, unpleasant, forward. She agreed.

Later that day, I got a text from the wife, "the Australian you met today," and I texted back that it was nice to meet them. She replied, glad that 'we connected' and I immediately blocked her number. Why? I don't know, just that it felt creepy.

Long ago, I entered a party with my boyfriend where the host gave each woman a long kiss at the door. We waited in line to greet him and hand over our coats. I stood helpless, being kissed. What was I thinking? Don't make a fuss? This is normal, you just don't know it. Plus, I had no training or experience or knowledge or conversation about this type of thing. Soon after, my boyfriend pointed out that the next woman to enter pulled away and said, "stop kissing me." I could have done that, he meant. I had no response.

When I was small, my Uncle Clarence liked to put his girl nieces, me and my sister, on his knee and give us a wet kiss. We didn't like it but we put up with it. My mother complained to me and my little sister that Uncle Clarence was French and she didn't like those kisses either. I guess she got them too. He was actually French Canadian, I think, but so what?

Now, after #MeToo, it's obvious. Women and girls are preyed upon by some men, and we don't have to put up with it. But at the time, and even today, on a sunny October day in Venice, I forgot my own agency.

How do I remember? For next time? I'm in my seventies, for God's sake. When will they stop kissing without permission? Only when told, apparently.

I feel like I've let my side down, women and girls. I feel stupid but not as embarrassed and ashamed as I felt years ago. No, I just feel sad that this is true, that I accepted unwanted sexual contact – for that's what those kisses were – rather than make a fuss, rock the boat, make a man who was being nice to me feel bad. Don't make others feel bad, is that it? At my own expense, my diminished self, intruded upon, private space invaded?

LIGHTEN UP

Noodling around on an alumni website one afternoon, I noticed an increasing number of my high school classmates had joined the site. It was a big anniversary year: forty-five years since we'd taken the Pomp and Circumstance walk in upstate New York. The class of '64 was due for a reunion. We hadn't had one in ten years, and I didn't want to wait another ten. I had a nice life in another state, with grown kids, and I was curious to see where my friends had ended up.

I sent a short note to a few names I recognized on the site, including my high school crush. He responded within minutes.

"Oh, ma-a-a-a-an," he wrote. "It's so good to see your smiling face again."

We emailed back and forth, and before long, he posed the question that was on my mind.

"Wouldn't it be great to have a reunion?"

Back and forth messages continued, until I sent a group email to everyone in our class on the website: Would any of them come to a high school reunion?

The Yes replies came quickly. I appointed us the "organizing committee," and we were off. Eight of us planned the whole thing in three months, from California, New Hampshire and Pennsylvania, by email and with two "on the ground" in our hometown.

My heart sang as we became reacquainted. Everyone sounded just like they did way back when. The bubbly cheerleader sent chirpy notes with lots of exclamation points and capital letters. The brainy science guy sent complicated explanations of lamely intellectual puns. But all too soon, the emails took a different turn.

Ethnic "jokes" and "politically incorrect" humor flooded my e-mailbox. Slams against liberals. Slurs on the President, Democrats, global warming experts, and Al Gore. Strangely, nobody shared any anti-conservative humor with me.

At first, I deleted the messages. They didn't stop, and whenever I opened and read one, I felt sad and disappointed. Our happy dance was over. After one friend's joke included a full frontal nude photo of a woman, I asked him to take me off his email list. He apologized to the whole group, sparking a flurry of replies about "lightening up" because "a good laugh never hurt anyone."

One woman forwarded messages almost every day. The topics varied: Nobody says Merry Christmas anymore; Hispanic immigrants are criminals; the government takes your money and gives it to lazy people. Beneath the words, I sensed a layer of simmering anger and resentment that brought down my energy level, my vibration, and my sense of inner peace.

But we had a reunion to plan. I needed to open messages, and it was sometimes hard to tell from the subject line which ones were related to the upcoming party and which were just another political tirade. When that same woman forwarded a long "joke" about building a wall around all the countries in the Middle East and flooding them, I sent a reply.

"This is so mean-spirited," I said. "I have a sponsored sister in Afghanistan. Please take me off your list for forwarded jokes."

"No, it wasn't," she wrote back. "I do not have a mean spirit, as you so tactfully put it. Ethnic jokes have been around forever; comedians tell them all the time, even when their own ethnicity is the butt of their jokes."

She went on to say her former husband was cousin to a mutual friend, "and when we got together the Italian and Polish jokes flew." I wondered: Was this meant to prove to me it was all right? "Lighten up, it's a JOKE," she concluded.

As if this weren't enough, one of my Facebook friends posted a racist comment on his "Wall" about the President. When I told him I found it offensive, he replied with a verbal attack on "closed-minded liberals" like me and asserted his right to speak against the President because he was a combat medaled Vietnam veteran.

"Good riddance," he shot back at me when I removed him from my list of friends. "You are a *nut*!"

Sadly, I think I know how he feels. Reading anger and hate-filled diatribes, and then mass mailing them to friends, calls for a certain level of resentment. There once was a day when I plotted to get even with those who had hurt me. I searched for the best words to wound them, to prove how right I was. Although the words were my own and not those of a biased website, using them to attack someone did not make me feel better. It just left me angry and self-righteous, unable to hear any voice but my own.

A few days later, I decided I wanted to be open, to have a dialogue. We of the Scorpio signs of the zodiac love to dig into the depths of meaning. I laid out the evidence for my side of the story. I thought it was incumbent upon me to explain to my classmates why I didn't agree with what they said. I believed I really had a chance to open their hearts. But nothing changed.

Frustrating, isn't it? But that's the good news. My classmates are annoyed by the "politically correct" because they are losing the battle. It's no longer acceptable to tell racial or ethnic jokes. They're on the way out.

If you ask me, this whole thing is a very good sign of our progress as a people. Frankly, I feel lighter just thinking about it.

BULLIES, THEN AND NOW

George, my elderly neighbor, is not well-liked. He has a reputation for being a grouch, but in the six years we've lived in our townhouse community, my husband and I have tried to be friendly and cordial with everyone. When George-from-across-the-street said that Sam-from-next-door hated him because he was Jewish, and that Sam's wife Gert was crazy, I said we wanted to get along with all our neighbors. For six years, I smiled and made nonpartisan sympathetic noises while Sam and George badmouthed each other. My husband counseled them, both men in their mid-eighties, to calm down before they had heart attacks. But this week, their feud entered my personal space.

My husband and I were about to get into our car for a day out, when George ambled by. We had a pleasant conversation about a bed he was buying his dog when out of the blue, George wheeled toward Sam's garage, right next to ours, and shouted, "What the hell are you lookin' at?" Sam was merely standing in his garage, perhaps giving George a dirty look. And for me, it was childhood all over again.

My dad verbally berated my mother, my sister and I for all kinds of minor transgressions. "What the hell" was a common prelude to a string of insults. My mother was a lousy cook, my sister and I made noise with our forks. My mother "had no friends." I "had no boyfriend." Honestly, the stuff he came up with to yell at us for almost makes me laugh today. Almost. Because it still hurts.

I have been through years of therapy. I have many self-help books. I have taken seminars on loving myself. And yet. In a second, all the protection I had built up around the scared little girl inside of me tumbled down at my feet.

One thing since childhood has changed. I did not remain silent. I did not cry. (Until later.) I yelled back.

"I don't care what your problem is, take it someplace else. I don't want you yelling in my driveway!" George turned on his heel and walked across the street, got in his car, and drove away. To buy the dog bed, no doubt.

I got into the passenger seat and prepared to drive away with my quiet husband. But Sam moved toward us and motioned for me to roll the window down. Before he could speak, I told him off too. "I don't care what the problem is with you two, I don't want to hear it. And I don't like being in the middle of it."

"I didn't say anything!" Sam protested.

"I know you didn't," I replied and rolled up the window. As we drove away, I let the tears fall. Tears of anger, yes, but also fear. I was yelling at George and Sam, and also at my dad. The man who terrorized my childhood with his words. He never hit us, but we lived in constant fear of his tirades. We never knew when he would blow, and that's why angry men terrify me still.

Later, on the treadmill at the gym, I saw the President of the United States on one of the TV screens and my stomach clenched. I flashed back to his campaign rallies. "Get the hell outta here!" "Throw 'em the hell out!" He's toned it down a lot, but all I need to see is his face or to hear his voice and my body reacts like the little girl in her father's house long ago.

"He's a bully," I thought. "The President and my neighbor are bullies." And I remembered my son's tormented middle school years. With undiagnosed ADHD, he had trouble sitting still in the classroom and learned differently. A neurological defect made his head dip when he walked and the mean kids called him "Cranker." When he was sixteen, some boys invited him outside for a birthday surprise: a beating about the body where bruises would not show. They blamed him for being so gullible, but he was just trying to be a good sport, to have friends. It was years before he got over this, and writing now, I realize he may not be over it yet. Like me, he may carry this hurt all his life.

After he graduated from college, he ran into one of the high school bullies at a convenience store. The young man apologized to him, and my son said it was a great feeling. It was a good, courageous and insightful thing that young man did, when he could have just slunk away. He made himself vulnerable, too, like my son had been. He admitted his sin and made amends.

I wonder if that will ever happen in my neighborhood. And in the wider world outside my door.

DANGER BOY

From the moment he is born, you try to keep him safe. You read the label of ingredients in a jar of baby food. You wonder if you can dust off that carrot he threw onto the floor and put it back on the tray of his highchair. You read magazine articles on how to keep him from doing drugs when he reaches middle school. You bone up on stranger danger and water safety and vaccination schedules. But it never occurs to you to protect him from a classmate with a crossbow.

Your son Darren was eleven. His father divorced you when he was only two, and you had a promising career with a major pharmaceutical company. You liked your job but it was an hour away from home. Bob, your ex-husband, lived nearby, and you shared custody but you didn't like each other much. You didn't talk about how to raise Darren. You didn't talk about values and religion and healthy food and exercise. You only discussed the logistics, practical things like what days to transfer him and his clothes, schoolbooks and toys, who would go to the school conference, and who would pay what for after school day care.

The year of the crossbow incident, Darren was aging out of day care. He was bored with the craft activities dreamed up by the teenaged counselors at the Y, and begged you to let him be on his own after school. He was a forgetful child, and you weren't comfortable with letting him go home alone. You weren't sure he was ready to take care of himself for the two or three hours before you got home from work. As a compromise, you hired Kenny, a 15-year-old boy who lived nearby to watch him in your apartment after school. Bob insisted on coming over to interview the boy as well.

Kenny was a polite slightly overweight kid, and you were impressed by his mature attitude about homework and snacks. Kenny's mom was pleased. He wanted to earn his own money but she felt he was too young to work at McDonald's or Seven Eleven.

None of you knew how dangerous this first job would turn out to be. On the afternoon you remember now, a classmate got off the school bus with your son and invited him over to play. Kenny met the bus and walked with Darren to his friend's apartment in the same complex. The new boy's name was Donny. At eleven, he was as chunky as Kenny and as tall. Inside his apartment, Donny tossed his books on the couch and strode to a hall closet. Your son and his sitter stood just inside the door, uncertain, as Donny turned around with a crossbow in his arms.

"I knew it wasn't something we should be playing with," Kenny told you later.

You loved him for taking your son out of there. But Donny came over later to play at your apartment, minus the crossbow. When he left, Darren discovered thirty-five dollars missing from his dresser drawer.

When you got home from work, Kenny told you what happened, and for the first and only time, you spoke with danger boy's mom on the phone.

"My Donny would never steal," she said. "But I will definitely talk to him about the crossbow. He knows he's not supposed to touch it."

After you disconnected, you were not satisfied. You wondered why she had a crossbow in her closet. You didn't wonder at a boy's curiosity.

Fast forward 27 years, and a Facebook friend messages you: "Neighbor from Granite Cove?" She has attacked a news article with the now grownup Donny's mug shot. You read in horror: "Man Charged in Girlfriend Death." Your eyes move down the page. Donny was arrested for strangling a woman in a motel, then trying to make it look like suicide before fleeing in her car while high on heroin. Arrested the next day at a local hospital, he'd been trying to check into a rehab program. He had previous convictions for robbery and theft and was being held without bail.

You message your grownup son. "Do you remember this guy?"

He answers, "Nobody who knew him at school is surprised," and you wonder what else he isn't telling you. What else did you not think to ask, what else did you not worry about and should have when you were a single mother trying so hard and never feeling like you knew what you were doing?

Darren is a good man, kind and compassionate, with a good job. But his childhood was rocky. He struggled to control his anger throughout his teen years. Many episodes as the target of bullies tore at his self-esteem, and he vented his frustration at his teachers, his parents, and even a few of his friends. You and your ex worried about his future. You felt responsible for his problems. You often felt helpless. But even then, there were things you just knew.

Your son would never kill someone. Never in a million years. You remember now how you knew that then. You don't notice you are holding your breath until you're dizzy.

You find a chair to support you, sit there and think of Donny's mother, so sure her son would never steal. You think about the mother of the girl you never knew. And the three young boys whose mothers loved them too. And now you know what you didn't when you read the labels on baby food jars: you can't control everything. You remember how hard you tried.

PART IV

HEARTSTRINGS

WE CAME FOR TOAST

He had over five hundred toasters in his kitchen and dining room, arranged above the cabinets, in bookshelves and across the deep windowsills of his huge Victorian home. He collected them at flea markets and antique fairs, many of which I attended with him and his friends, collectors of other oddities like light bulbs and cowboy boots. It wasn't that I was interested in toasters, or light bulbs, or even antiques. I wanted someone to love me.

His friends were weird, but I didn't care. I would have given myself up for a life with him, indeed gave up two years, but only two, in wasted effort.

We listened to classical music, went to dinner or a movie. He chose the date and activity, I went along. We did not fit. His kids were grown and I only met them once. I was divorced with a son, and he criticized my parenting. He didn't seem to like kids.

A closeted gay friend saw me crying over him and got the idea to make him jealous by kissing me where he could see us at a bar. We laughed at our secret, and it worked, but not enough to make us right for each other.

One day, after he and I had split, two colleagues convinced me to knock on his front door on the way to a meeting. They knew I missed him, and our route went right past his house.

"We came for toast," I said when he opened the door. He looked at me, then Helen, then Patty, and smiled his bemused smile. He suggested lunch, looking at Helen again, longer. She laughed and said we had no time. We scampered back to the car.

Patty said, "Now the ball is in his court. You reached out." He never reached back.

Today, I barely recognize the woman I was then, looking for love and tired of the search, lonely.

"We look at life in different ways," he said, explaining why he'd never love me. I wanted him, someone safe and secure, older, with a big house, even if it was full of toasters.

When I ended it, he told me he didn't miss my neediness, only the warm body in his bed. He asked out my best friend. She turned him down out of loyalty to me and also because she wasn't interested.

An old rickety toaster at a flea market today brings a smile of recognition for the woman I was then, open and loving – too much so. But I don't blame her for trying.

In a way, I owe him. Without that two-year exercise in futility, I might still be trying too hard to please, forgetting myself, forever on the doorstep, knocking.

A LIFETIME LATER

It's been forty-five years since I graduated from high school, forty-five years since my crush signed my yearbook with "love." He sat behind me in almost every class. In those days, we were assigned seats by last name and ours were very close together, alphabetically speaking. Every day, I twisted in my chair to ask him a question, crack a joke, borrow a pencil, make him smile at me. And every day, he told me, not unkindly, to turn around.

He wasn't the least bit interested in me. He liked another girl, although I didn't know it then. Once, I invited him to a graduation party and he accepted. The party turned out to be a crashing bore and I was painfully embarrassed. None of my friends – the "average kids," and none of his – the "most popular" students, was there. We were trapped in a house with the guest of honor's elderly Italian relatives and dorky cousins. What would he think of me now? On the spot, I couldn't come up with a thing to say or do.

He took me aside and spoke quietly into my ear. "Let's stay for an hour, then tell her we have another party to go to. And then we'll go to a movie." I don't remember the movie, but I can still feel my relief at his thoughtfulness, both to me and to our hostess.

I wasn't used to men like this. My father was a frustrated, verbally abusive man, and I was used to hearing him call my mother names. I was used to him criticizing just about everything I did, and my mother doing nothing to stop him, preoccupied as she was with saving the remaining scraps of her own self-respect.

After graduation, my crush and I went to nearby colleges, and one night he called to invite me to a fraternity weekend. His date was sick, he said, but he had tickets and would I go in her place? Of course, I would. At the first event of the weekend, a frat brother made a snarky comment about me being second choice and not quite up to my date's usual standard. I don't remember exactly what my friend said to him, but I recall the way the frat brother slunk away, embarrassed. For the first time in my life, someone stood up for me, and I never forgot it.

We didn't speak again for forty-five years, a lifetime. He joined the service, got married, became an architect, moved to California, had grandchildren. I got married, moved to the Philadelphia suburbs, became a librarian, had two sons, wrote a book. Last year, as we planned our high school reunion via email, I realized he and my husband share the same qualities. I ended up with the perfect man for me.

And over a beer at the reunion, I finally had the chance to tell him what it had meant to me, all those years ago, to be treated so gently and kindly by a boy who could so easily have broken my heart. One of the best things about getting older is finally finding the words to tell him that.

THIS IS A MOMENT OF SUFFERING

Next to the sticky-note on my standing desk stands a little blue angel about two inches tall. I like to stroke her rough stone dress with my thumb or rest a fingertip on the tiny blue heart she holds in both hands.

When I answer the doorbell and let her inside, Kathy's head is lowered over the bucket in her hand.

"You're early," I say. "Good morning!"

She gives me a thin smile. "Where would you like me to start?"

"Upstairs, I guess. We're still finishing up in the kitchen."

Once she is out of sight, the house is quiet, the two of us working in different rooms. I load the dishwasher and climb the stairs, wondering. Kathy is normally friendly, even loud. She always asks about my weekend or a recent holiday. Not today.

I find her in a bathroom, rooting around her bucket of sponges. She doesn't look up when I come closer.

"How was your weekend?"

"Okay." She straightens and begins to mop the floor. I don't move, sensing more will come. "Actually, I have to tell you something." She pushes her glasses up with one finger and takes a long deep breath. "My son passed away."

"Oh, no! Oh, Kathy, I'm so sorry!"

She nods but keeps her eyes low and begins to talk, standing in my bathroom. What was God thinking? Why can't he send him back? She's read the sticky-note on my desk, a quote from a self-help book: "This is a moment of suffering. Suffering is a part of life. May I have compassion for myself in this moment. May I give myself the comfort I need."

"I don't think I can do that," she says. "Give myself the comfort I need." This is her first cleaning job since the accident claimed her son's life. A fall in a warehouse broke his neck, leaving behind a one-year-old daughter and fiancé, plus eight brothers and sisters and his parents. Kathy's husband finds a quiet spot at work to cry alone, she says, as does her son at high school. We talk about guidance counselors and grief support groups.

She rubs at her arms, and I hug her, and when Steve gets home, I break the news. She thanks us for letting her talk, says keeping busy helps her cope. No obituary because she didn't want calls from his friends.

I remember my disbelief the day his father called to say our son attempted suicide, the way I repeated one word: What? What? Over and over, pleading for it not to be true. Thankfully he survived, but other sons among my friends did not. How random this is, how different we are, and how much alike.

"I know you're religious," Kathy, a devout Catholic, says. Is it because of my angel figurines? She is tall, strong-boned and works alone cleaning my entire townhouse in three hours. I feel stiff and old and sometimes go to the gym while she is working. "Good for you, she says, you want to stay in shape."

As she goes back to work, I walk into my office, wanting to do more to ease her pain. I read the sticky note quote beside the angel and revisit the moment I first saw her in a little art gallery in Lahaina. No. Not her. She is mine. I look around for something else. A card? An artificial flower? I have so many articles of beauty here: pictures, sayings, beads.

I spot another angel, a gift from Janice. It's not as nice and kind of hokey, like you'd find in a card store: big eyes and a floral ringlet on her head. Maybe that one. I go downstairs and quietly talk to Steve. He listens to me explain about the angels.

"Shall I give her the one I bought in Maui? The one I really like?"

"It's up to you," he says.

If I give her the big-eyed angel, I won't really miss it. She has Janice's energy, not mine.

I pick up my angel from Maui and stroke her skirt with my thumb. This one I love. This one has my energy, the compassion and care I feel when I look at her every day, when I hold her.

I hear Kathy downstairs, packing up to leave. I hurry down to her, beauty in my hand, and say, "I want to give you this."

TEMPORARY TEARS

I broke my hand in a moment of joy.

My son and husband were a feet away, watching football in our "sunken" family room. I had just placed three salmon fillets in a baking dish and slid them into the oven. We had moved into our new townhouse that fall, and I was still enjoying everything about it, especially the kitchen.

"Don't you just love this house," I exclaimed, throwing my arms into the air while stepping down to where they sat on the couch. My sock slid off the carpeted step and I hit my left hand on the wooden coffee table.

My son laughed, not realizing how bad it was. My husband asked if I was alright. "It really hurts," I cried, cradling the hand in my other one. It stung, it ached, it throbbed. “Ow, ow, ow,” I moaned, rocking back and forth.

“It’s probably just a sprain,” my husband said. “I’ll get some ice.”

The ice didn’t help, and we left for the urgent care center on the corner. The x-ray showed a fracture of the bone below my ring finger. We had to get the ring off, fast, the technician said, before my hand swelled. I insisted on doing it myself, reasoning I could at least control the pain. An appointment at the orthopedic doctor’s office followed. I was fitted, at 70, with my first ever plaster cast, and given instructions on how to wash, dress and manage the pain.

My unexpected winter vacation had begun. I couldn't write, drive, knit or quilt. Most of my favorite activities were now impossible.

After the initial shock and pain subsided, I welcomed holiday visitors to our new home, encouraging them to sign my purple cast with a silver Sharpie. Friends brought meals, took me to appointments, and in the case of my wonderful husband, blow-dried my hair. This wouldn't be so bad. I went from disbelief to denial in just a few days. Then reality set in.

My friends and family went back to school and work, and I was left with the business of healing. While I eagerly awaited the removal of my cast three weeks after my injury, I was not prepared for what I would see. My naked hand looked like a dead fish. I couldn't hold it up by itself. An ache deep inside the weakened muscles brought tears to my eyes, tears I didn't try to hide from the young doctor.

"I didn't know it would hurt so much," I sniffled.

"Well, you did break your hand," he said. His smile was gentle. "I guess we didn't prepare you enough."

He fitted me with a removable brace and sent me home for another three weeks of rest. At home, I sat in a chair, reading and weeping. I wish I could say each day was a little better, but it was more like the old "two steps forward, one step back" syndrome. My emotional state on some days had more to do with the slow progress of healing than with any physical pain.

I read spiritual and self-help books, visited inspirational websites, and talked my dear husband's ear off. I wanted to stop feeling sorry for myself. I wanted it now. But I had suffered a sudden and painful loss: my ability to function with two hands and to do so many things I missed. Couldn't I have some time to mourn?

When a loss is "only" temporary, we may not allow ourselves time to grieve. We mentally "slap ourselves upside the head," try to "suck it up," to remember how many worse situations other people are going through. We list our gratitudes and look for lighter moments. Some people watch funny movies or listen to comedy shows. It's not the end of the world, right? But how bad does the loss have to be to deserve a timeout for some personal attention? Aren't we allowed to grieve the "little things?"

I've always been a sensitive person. I feel things deeply. But even if I didn't, why not allow myself a day or two of tearful sadness? All the happy talk wasn't helping. I wiped my eyes (with my right hand) and read a good book. Some days, I watched a movie. Often, a redheaded woodpecker ate suet outside my window. I know because I gave myself time to sit and watch him. He didn't seem to care if I cried.

Now that I'm "all better," I still have that time.

I gave it to myself.

TWISTED

Twisted. Contorted. Distorted. Rotated. Warped. Coiled. Spiraled.

"Let's keep an eye on it," my pediatrician said. "It shouldn't be a problem until she's older." I was 14.

Every year, I stripped to the waist and bent over as a succession of young male doctors checked and rechecked the progress of my spinal curve. The blossoming of my developing teenaged body embarrassed me. The curve stayed the same, and no further treatment ensued.

My mother sewed my clothes, straight pins between her pursed lips, her throat making disapproving noises as she struggled to make a dress hang straight over my protruding left hip or tried to disguise my poking-out right shoulder blade. "Never wear a blouse tucked in," she said. "And never wear a belt."

For my wedding, a seamstress altered my four-hundred-dollar gown, to this day the most expensive dress I have ever bought, so that the line of pearl buttons marched straight up my back. Twenty years later, I noticed, looking over my photo in our wedding album, the buttons were fine, but my left hip jutted out to the side. My right shoulder blade poked out the white fabric at the back.

"Do you have scoliosis?" asked a woman at church, walking up the stairs behind me. "Don't ever wear that dress again."

I was teaching at a retirement home when a retired fashion model walked up and touched my shoulder. "Just one shoulder pad, here, and your shirt would fall perfectly."

So much advice. Well-meaning, to be sure. And if I tried to follow it all? Daily checking how I looked, knowing there was little I could do to change my shape, was quite simply exhausting. Yet, I have never wanted corrective surgery. I never wore a brace. For most of my life, the problem was merely cosmetic.

When I began to write creatively, my curving spine became my metaphor for adjusting to the twists and turns of life. Just as my spine made me look and feel off kilter, my early life felt as wrong as a badly fitting dress. I learned to be quiet but not too quiet, to smile and not show anger, to not trust my feelings, and to make myself smaller than I already was. The messages went on and on. Go to secretarial school instead of college. (Stay home with us.) Turn down that scholarship to grad school. (Don't quite your day job, we need the money.)

Finally, life as it was presented to me became so uncomfortable, I began to take slow careful steps to explore a better path, one that was tailored by me. Thanks to other women, my church, and friends and family who loved me as I was, and all the people who barely noticed my deformity, I found my way. Physical therapy and yoga managed the pain and psychotherapy healed the emotional wounds, leaving scars I could use to grow in confidence and empathy.

Now I am an old woman. The world no longer expects me to conceal my deformity. Yes, viewed from behind, I am still off kilter. But face forward, I am steady on.

I WANT TO GO HOME

Her little fingers fumbled with a sheet of yellow construction paper. Her white camp T-shirt, too big, topped her ruffled skirt. Her bright pink sneakers matched the headband in her jet-black hair.

In the high-ceilinged activities room, nineteen other kids, ages five to twelve, sat at tables with paper and scissors, learning origami. We were all learning, even the adult volunteers like me. Our teacher, a middle-aged Chinese American woman, was unbelievably adept. I, on the other hand, was having a hard time of it.

When I answered the call last spring for volunteers at a Chinese Culture Camp, I envisioned a fun-filled week with little children. Instead, it turned into quite the unexpected challenge. The arts and crafts were so complicated, I felt inept from the start. The only thing this retired librarian was good at was untangling yoyo strings and handing out supplies and snacks.

I work best when I have explicit instructions. Do A, then B. "Help them with this" was not remotely clear enough for me, and that was all the training I got. The first morning, I wanted to go home. I thought of saying I felt sick. The second day, I mentally practiced, but did not use, another excuse: I forgot, there is somewhere else I have to be.

The third day, the children sang "Twinkle, Twinkle Little Star" in Chinese, complete with hand signs, and I was hypnotized into staying. I wanted to be with them, to bask in the joy on their openly eager faces. At snack time, I put out bags of pretzels, helped little hands peel oranges and passed out water bottles. I talked with the other volunteers and the high school boys who came to demonstrate the Chinese yoyo.

Still, no day was easy for me. Although I was good at handing out crayons, origami made me feel stupid. The teacher deftly showed us how to fold the paper then moved on to the next table. Although I concentrated hard, her fingers flew before my eyes. My folds all went in the wrong directions. I followed her around the room watching her demonstrate over and over how to turn ordinary construction paper into beautiful flowers.

"Can you help me?" The little girl with the pink headband asked.

Uh oh. Do not fail this child. Breathe and focus. My hands worked slowly, carefully turning precise folds of my paper into... a crumpled ball of yellow. She threw her own paper down on the table.

"I want to go home." *Me too.* But I was one of the grownups, the people who are supposed to know how to do things. My face felt hot.

"Can I make something else?" she said.

"Of course," I said. "You can make anything you want."

"I need scissors," she said. I could help with that. She took them from my hand, snipped here and there at the folded paper, and finally opened it to show me a lacy pattern of holes.

"Can I hang it up?" The walls and windows already held a multitude of partially completed coloring pages and paper snowflakes autographed in crayon.

"Yes, you can."

"I need some tape," she said. I could help with that, too. I held the chair she climbed to hang her work as high in the window as her little arms could reach. Sunlight poured through the holes of her design.

"Beautiful," I said. She smiled. I believe she thought I meant the paper.

PART V

DISCOVERIES

FRESH OFF THE BOAT

Imagine your cold feet inside damp socks, sticking to the linings of your sneakers. Imagine jumping not quite far enough to miss the puddles on a busy Italian street. Rain drips off your eyeglasses as you try to read the map your cruise ship provided. You want to find a famous covered market, the one your guidebook said was "one of the largest, most historical and most beautiful covered markets in Europe." *Mercato Centrale di Livorno* - The Livorno Central Market - is located in an 18th-century art nouveau-style building on *Aurelio Scali Saffi* right next to the Royal Canal. But where is the Royal Canal? Your husband insists he knows the way but you are skeptical. You just want to get inside, get warm, dry your feet.

It's the first morning of your 30th anniversary Mediterranean cruise, and you have arrived at your first stop since leaving the port of Civitavecchia. You've never heard of it but then you've never heard of Livorno, either, but here you are. It's been raining since the shuttle from the dock dropped you off in the center of the shopping district, but there's no way you would have stayed on board, luxurious though your ship truly was. You've never been to Italy and you only have this day.

You gaze longingly at the umbrellas and warm hats of pedestrians, before you duck into an information center where a nice woman behind the counter shows you the way to the market, in English, on another map. Go outside, she says, turn left and there it will be.

But the streets spread out like the crooked spokes of a wheel, bent out of shape and snaking between buildings just tall enough to block your view. Which one is the left she meant you to take? It could be one of three. Your husband says he knows. It's that one. You follow him and right there across the street is a small brightly lit shop. Through the big window, you see an artful display of knit hats. You scoot inside to try on a soft purple one, and you buy it - only 6 euros. It feels good on your head. You see your reflection in a mirror, looking fashionable and you are cheered.

You walk on, trying different streets, with no covered market in sight. You tell your husband your socks are wet, you want to ask someone else for directions, and maybe the market isn't going to happen. A pastry shop beckons – don't they always? - and you pull open the glass door and step inside. Nobody at the counter understands what you are saying. Frustration grips your forehead and all you want to do is get warm and dry. Not even a pastry will make you happy now.

From somewhere behind you, a male voice speaks. "Where do you want to go?"

"The covered market," you say. "*Mercato Centrale*." You show him on the map.

"Why do you want to go there? It's nothing to see." He is fortyish, dark-haired and handsome. A short pretty brunette is at his side, smiling up at you.

You tell them you just want to be indoors, to see something you can walk to. You remember the next item on your list. Perhaps the Modigliani Museum?

"Ah, it is beautiful," he says and turns to the front of the store, where rain sheets down outside the glass. "*Mamma mia*!" he says, waving his arms. He starts to give directions but his wife interrupts and they argue back and forth in Italian. Clueless, you watch their hands as they wave toward the window, left, right, up in the air. They shake their heads and laugh while you stand there, wondering.

All at once he says, "Come, I will take you there. My car is just outside." He gestures toward the door, his wife nodding and smiling. You look at your husband. He looks at you. Imagine the headline: American Tourists Kidnapped in Italy.

The man sees your silent exchange. "You can trust me," he says. "I'm a lawyer." Everybody laughs and you shrug and follow this nice Italian couple outside and sure enough, his car is right there at the curb. He gestures to the car seat in the back. "*Per i bambini!*" His wife motions you in beside the car seat while your husband gets in front with her husband, the driver. "It's not far," he says, and launches into a lecture. "Livorno is a very important port…." His wife rolls her pretty brown eyes at you and giggles. You are squished together in the back seat, so close, but you are not concerned. She points at your chest.

"*Il nave?*" You shake your head and say you are sorry, you don't understand. "Boat?" she says, pointing back toward the harbor.

"Yes, yes," you say, so happy to connect. You feel a pulse of energy passing between you. "*Si, si! Il nave*!" Your heads bob rapidly up and down and you laugh together.

Imagine you are off the boat in more ways than one, this rainy morning. More than a hundred years ago, all of your grandparents and even your husband's dad left this very same continent from another harbor, headed for New York. They left the only home they'd ever known for a new life that was only a hopeful dream.

Yesterday, you flew from New York to Rome in eight hours, a third of a day. You stepped aboard a luxury liner for something they likely never dreamed of - a vacation on a ship. Their boat trip took weeks; they were probably seasick and traveled in steerage. There were no waiters, and no violins at dinner. Nobody gave them a map.

But they gave you this. This life in which you step off a boat back in Europe. They might wonder why you'd do such a thing. You meet kind people who speak a strange language, people they would probably have stayed away from, not knowing the safety that is your life. You can't blame them for that.

The young lawyer is right. The ride to the museum is short. He drops you off at the entrance and with his wife, wishes you a nice day. *Grazie,* you say, and you part in the universal language of nods and smiles.

At the museum, you finally get warm. You are fascinated by the work of an artist who lived only 35 years and died of tuberculosis one hundred years ago, yet gained the esteem of his contemporaries, including Pablo Picasso. Livorno is his birthplace. "Modigliani knew how to soak up influences from everyone, especially where to find new life and inspiration in the non-European and non-traditional world," the museum's curator wrote. "As a sea-faring man, someone who lived in a city with a harbour, the port of Livorno, he understood that you can't live there without encountering people coming into the port from elsewhere..."

You don't care about your socks anymore. That night, you hang them to dry in your cabin's tiny bathroom. You imagine the story you will tell.

NOTES FROM AN AMERICAN ISLAND

A rickety yellow school bus jolts along an unpaved road, thick green foliage brushing the windows on either side. I think of the movie Jurassic Park. People living here are descended from freed slaves. They are not dinosaurs. Their history, if they can help it, will not become extinct, even if that means sharing it with a busload of older white tourists.

South of Savannah and north of Jacksonville, a glistening bead in the chain of Sea Islands, Sapelo was home to West African slaves, brought here in chains to grow rice and cotton and other crops for their owners. Their descendants established several communities on the island, still reachable only by boat, but only one, Hog Hammock, remains.

Maurice, our affable bus driver and guide on this late April morning, is a strapping Black man in a Pittsburgh Steelers cap. I imagine him in another life, playing professional football, as he apologizes for potential lapses into Geechee, the Creole language developed here in the 18th century. He tells us the Saltwater Geechee were slaves on the Spalding and Reynolds plantations. Only about seventy of their descendants remain, a small, dedicated band determined to preserve Hog Hammock, the last Geechee settlement still occupied after the Reynolds company lured settlers to live in one small area on the island's southeastern shore.

At a picnic table behind the general store, Maurice's mother, Cornelia Bailey, signs her memoir. *God, Doctor Buzzard and the Bolita Man,* about growing up on Sapelo in the 1940s and 50s, and becoming a griot or storyteller. In a building across the dirt road, in the Sapelo Island Cultural and Revitalization Society, a tiny older woman in a straw hat and shirtwaist dress tells more island stories. "It's the woman on the ferry," I whispered to my husband, never having guessed she was on her way to work.

Maurice takes us past modest homes with television, cable and phone lines but no cell phone access. There is one general store and bar, and one gas station on the island. All supplies are ferried in or brought over on barges, which is fine with the Geechee. Developers would change their island, Maurice tells us, making it unaffordable. Even the state of Georgia's conservation efforts threaten to absorb the little private property that remains.

Maurice introduces a young male relative who wants to speak to us. He's just moved here from Brooklyn and his passionate love for the history of Sapelo Island pins me to his every word: words like "oppression" and "racism," spoken with an assertive self-confidence quite different from the soft-spoken Maurice and Cornelia. As soon as he stepped off the bus, Maurice apologized. At the first opportunity for a private conversation, I ask him why. Some tourists had complained. They didn't like being "lectured." The young man was "too political."

I tell Maurice there is no need for apology. Real people's lives are not a museum display. History is messy, complex, untidy. And sometimes uncomfortable. I liked that young guy. Maurice smiles a gentle smile, and thanks me but I'm not sure he'll heed my words. Tourists are important here. I can see that.

That afternoon, he drives us to the Reynolds Mansion, a plantation house with endless rooms and a bowling alley. In the nearby woods, ramshackle slave cabins and an obscure little slave cemetery cast a shadow over my heart.

At the end of the day, we arrive at a quiet beach where Maurice's family pulls up in a van and begins unloading baskets of food.

"What's in this?" I ask, taking a bite of moist sweet cake. A Black woman narrows her eyes, as if expecting criticism. It makes me sad, so I smile and say, "It's delicious!"

A young Black man at her side says, "It's a Sapelo Secret!" and everybody laughs.

All too aware of our differences now, knowing I was soon to leave on the ferry, as part of the privileged class who pay to see how these people live, I wonder. Am I gawking at their lives for my own entertainment? Or respectful of their lives and culture? Maybe some of both.

After our picnic, we walk on soft white sand beside grassy dunes strewn with sea cucumbers and shells. On the far horizon, shrimp boats float against a blue sky with puffy white clouds. I breathe a silent prayer for the Geechee to hold out as long as they can.

THEY CALL THEMSELVES INDIANS

Our busload of senior citizens came to a stop on a dirt road in New Mexico, unsure of what to expect. After the balloon fiesta in Albuquerque, and a couple of days in Santa Fe, we were bound for lunch in Tesuque pueblo, at the home of Louie Pena, a Native American conservationist and river guide.

One of New Mexico's smallest pueblos, with a population of about 400, Tesuque has been in its present location in the foothills of the Sangre de Cristo Mountains for over 800 years. Louie would meet us in the road, because the bus was too big to travel down his street. No photos were permitted, a tribal decision. We would see the place framed only by our preconceptions, and I knew I had a few of those.

My Polish grandparents came to North America in the 1890s, welcomed for their labor if not for their ethnicity. They were, in fact, recruited to work in rug, broom and glove factories. Louie's people have been here much longer. We stood on what is left of their land, most of it taken from them by white settlers before my own people arrived. An oblivious little white girl, I watched Tonto and the Lone Ranger on a black and white TV. I didn't learn about the genocide of Native peoples – not at school, at home, at church, or in the news. Not anywhere. But I know about it now. History is being rewritten to include the uncomfortable truth, and I knew it as I stood on that dirt road in Tesuque, squarely between an ancient unfamiliar culture and the dominant one I know so well.

Standing tall in the bright October sunshine, Louie described the traditional feast his wife had prepared, then led us down a path through a small field. We walked over a dry ditch on a makeshift bridge of boards, passing an old TV tube and other unrecognizable-to-me appliance parts in the weeds. The neighborhood lacked the type of landscaping my friends and I spend bundles of money on each spring and fall. We passed no ornamental plants in pots, no hanging baskets on porches. Dogs who might be German shepherds sniffed our legs and hands, tails wagging. No leashes, no barking. Though people give them names,

Louie said, and feed and pet them, they stay outside. We filed past a trampoline and a toddler's plastic riding toy in the yard, and Louie joked the toys were "not for me, for my grandkids."

Native art adorned the walls inside his home – baskets, paintings, rattles and feathers - and Native objects – dolls, pots, and dishes - filled a glass curio cabinet in a corner near the TV. Louie said he liked to watch the Boston Red Sox, and we all relaxed a little.

An enormous bear head looked down from the living room wall. Louie told us how he killed that bear as it stalked the village when he was only 14, while we devoured forkfuls of shredded chicken, potato salad and a hot corn dish I wish I had the recipe for. As he talked, his wife Serena served the food with quiet grace. Two of her thirteen grandchildren, a boy and a girl, moved expertly and quietly around the large open kitchen, emptying pots and filling serving bowls.

We sat on picnic benches in rapt attention as Louie passed around jars of dried herbs, his medicine. He talked about his classes in sustainable living, encouraging us to love our "Earth Mom." I've forgotten most of what he said, but I remember the sense of comfort he and his family created. I didn't want to leave.

Before meeting Louie's family, I believed indigenous Americans lived sad and poor lives, confined to reservations. I thought they were mostly alcoholic, starving, and ineffective protestors against oil and gas pipelines. But in the pueblo, I saw self-confident people promoting a healthy future while teaching their children to have pride in their culture. Louie and his family take tourists on Feast and Float rafting trips, teaching about ecology and serving natural Native foods. I thought of them later as I made my own soup and sorted laundry at home, doing the little things that make up my comfortable life.

I live as an elder Anglo woman in an increasingly diverse country, and I am determined to stay awake and aware. I want to know more. On the internet, I read about the tension between the Natives and Anglos over a plan to build a casino near the Santa Fe Opera, and about Indians charging access fees to Anglo people with homes on Native land. I read about the protests at the Santa Fe Plaza where I posed for a photo, and where the Spanish conquest of the Indians is celebrated every year.

Louie and all the tribal people we met in New Mexico called themselves Indians, but I wanted to distance myself from the Cowboys and Indians ethos of my youth, when we thought we knew who the bad guys were: *not us.* I continued to use the term I believed to be politically correct: Native Americans.

Back home, I discovered that the U.S. government coined the term in the late 20th century and that 50% of tribal people in the American West call themselves Indians. Many prefer the name of their particular tribe: Pueblo, Navaho, Ute, Zuni, Apache, Comanche. Louie Pena is Tewa.

Like many others, I often feel compelled to form a strong opinion about matters I don't fully understand. I don't know how Louie and his family feel about the protests or the casinos or the access fees. Or why they don't care about landscaping their neighborhood. I don't know how much I have assumed about them. I only know my visit to Tesuque changed my perception of tribal peoples and reminded me, at my advanced age, to listen and learn and prepare to be surprised. Now to sign up for that rafting trip…

LIBRETTO DECAFFEINATO

In a tiny coffee shop in Bologna, on a mild October afternoon, I ask the sixtyish man behind the counter for a coffee.

"*Americano decaffeinato, per favore*!" I say it loud because it's Italian and I love to hear myself speak it, to say the words Signora taught me in class so many years ago. Not these actual words. I looked them up in Duolingo. But all Italian words remind me of her greeting me with a cheerful "*Ciao*!"

I love to practice different languages, and I never miss a chance, though I sometimes confuse people. My friends and I are visiting Tuscany and I've been sick. But today my body feels rested and light, and the sun is warm and bright, and I am with a good friend.

Decaf, my usual, sounds like washing, like scratching. But here, in the land of opera, it becomes a drink melodic. Everything we say here, everything we hear, is music. Every ancient, round-voweled word is a melody and everyone a singer.

"*Piccolo*?" the counterman asks. "*Espresso*?"

"*No piccolo*," I say, waving my finger from side to side. Too small. I don't expect an American style mug, but a cup, at least, will do. He nods and smiles.

"*DECAFFEINATO*," I repeat, loud and emphatic. I must be sure. No coffee, my doctor said, while recovering from Covid. Even on the best of days, caffeine gives me heart palpitations and upsets my stomach. But I do love the smell and the taste. And the little buzz.

"Mi dispiace, no parlo italiano bene!"

"Ah, ha, ha, ha, ha!" Five beats, like the tenor in an opera. "I don't speak *inglese* well," he sings, passing me a steaming cup. The warm dark smell reaches my nose: so good, so familiar, even without the buzz.

My companion speaks to this man who is now our friend. "Just coffee, regular coffee," she says, and he sings to her, too.

"*Caffe normale*!" We all three laugh and share a joke – is it a joke? - across the counter, across the sea of our separate coffee-linked lives. I see us on stage at the Met. He wears a white apron and sings to me. "Two euro-o-o-s!"

My fingers do a little fumbling dance inside my coin purse. I sigh an impatient, embarrassed sigh. My hand passes two gold coins into his.

"*Grazie!*" his deep voice sings. He glides away from me, across the stage to serve my friend. I sidestep to the tip jar, place my hand over the open top and release two small coins that ring like tiny bells against the glass.

"*Ciao,*" my alto floats toward him. With a little wave, I exit stage left, and settle onto a blue metal chair outside. My friend takes a seat opposite me and our hands close around our warm cups on the sky-blue table. I sip the familiar brew. It warms my lips, my throat, my belly.

The fear, the worry, the sickness of the past week dissolve in the warm Italian sun. The curtain rises, and caffe in hand, my soul takes a bow.

REDISCOVERING THE OLD COUNTRY

When I was growing up in a Polish neighborhood in upstate New York, I wasn't so interested in the Old Country. My grandparents immigrated to America at the turn of the 20th century, and although my grandpa told me about the ducks on the farm near Warsaw where he lived as a boy, he was, by and large, a quiet man. The Old Country was, well, old, and we were living in the new postwar era in the United States. My parents wanted to move on after World War II, the Depression, my dad's Navy service in the Pacific, and my mother's hard factory labor. Like most of their friends, they wanted to be as all-American as they could possibly manage.

"We don't dress like DP's," my mother often said, code for displaced people coming from refugee camps in

Eastern Europe to the U.S. in old-fashioned clothes. Their English was broken, and although some moved into our hometown, we were embarrassed to be connected with them in any way.

Yet just like their parents, Mom and Dad sent me to a Polish Catholic school. We also attended a Polish Catholic church in a neighborhood where streets had names like Gorski and Pulaski. We ate kielbasa on Easter morning and danced the polka at weddings. We listened to clarinet and accordion records by Polish-American bands from Chicago on Sunday morning radio shows.

Our culture was a unique combination of ethnic pride and selective memory. No one I knew wanted to see the Old Country. That was the place where poverty choked you until you left, if you could. It was the place where cities had turned to rubble, and where Communists watched your every move, looking for any excuse to send you off to Siberia.

Mothers we knew packed up secondhand clothing, toothpaste, shampoo, and candy to send to family back in Poland. My family didn't have anyone left there, but my mom still contributed boxes of these items to the parish church for shipping.

In those days, the Poland in our minds was dust-poor, gray, and tragic. But its people who came here were better educated than my ancestors, albeit worse dressed.

We laughed nervously at Polish jokes. Even President Reagan told one, so they had to be okay. It was important to laugh at yourself here in America; we who felt the sting were being too sensitive. We tried to toughen up.

Somewhere along the way, all that changed. I got tired of laughing at my heritage. I wanted to know who I really was. And I wanted to claim the whole package, not just the sanitized version of my grade school teachers, who exhorted us to sing a Polish anthem "loud enough for the Russians to hear."

I am descended from a flat country, easily conquered and divided, a place with no name for all of the 19th century. My DNA goes back to a place, where in 44 years of atheist totalitarian rule, not one church closed its doors. Its strands tie me to the old men, women, and teenagers who crawled through Warsaw's sewers in 1944, desperate to take back their country from Nazi occupation. Both sides of my family have roots in Torun, Poznan, and Wojtowa, a village southeast of Krakow. I have a funny-sounding, hard-to-spell last name, thanks to my Polish-American husband, added to my equally hard-to-pronounce maiden name.

Sadly, my people also came from the land where millions of people, mostly Jews, were exterminated. Though many Poles hid and rescued them, many did nothing out of fear for their families' lives. And many reacted out of the anti-Semitism they learned as children. Some Poles even killed Jewish survivors returning home after the war.

Because of this, I traveled to Poland this summer with Elderhostel – an educational tour group for people over 55 – anticipating equal doses of pride and shame. At Auschwitz, I listened to a young Polish guide quote the words of German anti-Nazi theologian Martin Niemoller: "When they came for the Jews, I said nothing."

The next morning, Robert Gadek, a Jagiellonian University graduate, told the story of Jews in Poland, with none of the denial or self-justification I have heard among Polish Americans. He started a Jewish cultural festival that 30,000 people attended last year. He and the many people we met there were happy, purposeful, busy, and so proud that the fall of Communism started here. They were not embarrassed to be Polish. They were hopeful.

Much hope can be found in Poland's musical traditions. A Chopin concert welcomed us to our first evening in Warsaw 200 years after his birth. Opera songs bid us goodbye on our last evening in a castle lovingly restored by a young archeologist and his wife. And in between, at Wdzydze, the costumes, smiles, and lilting melodies of the folk musicians seemed to reach deep into my past, connecting me to the place where loving grandparents, aunts, and uncles also shared a bond.

Now back home in the United States, friends smile indulgently at my correct Polish pronunciation: 'Krah-Koov' as opposed to the soft and Anglicized 'Crack-cow.' I tell them I prefer the hard Polish consonants and long broad vowels. I think about the signs for Piwo, Kawiernia, Taverna, and Ksiazki that we drove by, trying to grasp the meaning behind their names.

Like cracking a secret code I forgot I knew, my first trip to my grandfather's homeland opened up a new understanding of him, my people, and myself.

THIRTY-TWO WORDS FOR PEACE

It was a blue-sky summer evening and I bounced on my heels and grinned. At seventy, I had finally made it to Paris. My husband and I eagerly waited in line to climb the Eiffel Tower. But the line wasn't moving.

"I'm hungry," I said, hoping for a view from the restaurant on the second level.

"Me too," said Steve. "We'll be up there just in time for sunset."

At the ticket window, a Middle Eastern family waved their arms in the air. Nearby, a handful of Japanese tourists milled around wearing puzzled expressions. Then a man in a business suit appeared, shouting first in English, then other languages.

"The Tower is closed temporarily! You may wait at least an hour here or proceed to the exit!"

Steve and I exchanged a glance. Hundreds of tourists murmured around us. Nobody smiled.

I looked back at the entrance where a guard in a security trailer had peered into my open backpack before I stepped out, excited and happy. Now the entire atmosphere had changed.

That same afternoon, we had walked down the Champs de Mars, named for the God of War, to see twelve glass panels engraved with the word Peace in 32 languages. Built for the millennium, the plan was to dismantle them after three months but they were still standing.

After a short walk from the glass panels, we stepped into the trailer, paid the admission fee for the Eiffel Tower, and proceeded to a small doorway. We were used to the drill back home, at the Empire State Building, the county courthouse and every airport - open your purse, lift your arms, remove your jacket – and with rueful glances as our eyes met, we complied. Built as a temporary structure for the 1889 World's Fair, the Tower was one of the most famous sights in the world, and an obvious target for terrorists.

After the unexpected announcement, we – and probably other couples with romantic dinner plans -

wondered if we should stay. All at once, soldiers with assault rifles and stern faces strode up and began going through everyone's bags. I felt a shiver of fear. Another man in a suit rushed up and spoke to the soldiers, who then moved to close the gates. One soldier turned to the crowd.

"You must exit across the plaza!" His face and his voice conveyed high alert and we knew there would be no more questions.

"Let's go," Steve said, taking my arm. We crossed back to the entrance with hundreds of people speaking into cell phones. I never thought to ask anyone for information in my high school French. The police looked much too busy to approach, and the eyes of the soldiers were hard, unblinking.

"What do you think it is," I asked.

Steve shook his head and shrugged. "No idea."

But, of course we had an idea. We watched the news. We knew about the coordinated attacks here the previous November, when over 100 people were killed at a football match, cafes and the Bataclan theater. But on this lovely summer evening, we didn't speak of it, as if saying the words might make it happen again. To us.

At least we were together. To the right of the trailer, tourists crowded before three open gates. A man shouted "Men!" and pointed left, then "Women!" and flung his arm to the right. Why were they separating us? My footsteps slowed and I thought of holding back but the crowd surged forward, carrying me along.

"See you outside!" I called to Steve, as he disappeared into the surge. But my promise was no comfort. I was alone in a crowd in a foreign country. I reminded myself to breathe and looked through the black iron bars of the fence for a sign of my husband on the street outside. When I was almost at the gate, a uniformed woman pushed her palm hard against my chest.

"You wait!" she shouted, then ushered a woman with a young girl through ahead of me. She patted my body from head to toe and examined my backpack, the same one I had opened for inspection on the way in. Trembling, I kept my expression sober so she'd have no reason to hold me back.

At last, I stood next to Steve on the sidewalk outside, catching my breath. In the street, police cars careened to a stop, and sirens blared in that high-pitched scream we knew from foreign films. Enough, I thought, wanting to get away. I pulled on Steve's arm.

"Let's find a restaurant. I'm starving."

We walked toward our hotel as more police cars screeched to a halt across the intersection, closing off the street behind us. I exhaled my tension as we left the commotion behind.

At the first bar along the way, we sipped cold beers, devoured hot mussels and shared our admiration for the businesslike French police. As I sat back and watched the people of Paris go about their evening, I was overcome by tenderness. For them, and for us. Yes, this kind of thing happened back home, but I'd never been so close before, never seen such calm in the face of danger. I held Steve's hand across the table, grateful beyond measure.

Back at the hotel, I checked the news online.

"Eiffel Tower Evacuated!" French authorities were calling it a false alarm by a new employee who mistook a drill for the real thing. The next day, I read that a backpack or "suspicious package" had caused the evacuation. Whatever the reason, a new reality had set in, dusting our visit with sadness.

Early last year, French officials announced plans to build an eight-foot bulletproof glass wall around the Eiffel Tower. In the new millennium, hate can kill without warning, even on beautiful summer evenings. Nearby, twelve panes of glass stand engraved with our longing.

WIDE OPEN SPACES

Driving from San Marcos to Austin on a wide ribbon of highway, cars coming toward me took forever to get close. I could see ahead for miles. It was a new sensation, terribly interesting. And terrifying. I would see trouble coming and have plenty of time to run but trouble would see me too. There was no shelter here.

The next day, I left the six-lane highway to drive beside it on the access road, closer to the fast-food restaurants and strip malls along one side, places where I could stop whenever I wanted.

I was almost an hour late for lunch because Jane's directions assumed I'd be driving the interstate. I pulled into a business park and stopped a mailman to find the way. Get back on the highway, he said. When I finally arrived at the restaurant, everyone had ordered. A few women said they were sorry I was late. Jane said, I gave her perfectly good directions, but she refused to use them, her New Zealand accent clipping her words, sharp.

I know, I said, I just don't like the interstate. You're out there in the open in the middle in the sun, nothing to touch on either side. Adrift, no boundaries at all. They looked at me, bemused. As if openness could produce anxiety. Imagine.

The next day, as I drove to another meeting, I listened to the Dixie Chicks sing "Wide Open Spaces." I pictured them singing about the great expanse of the Texas landscape, not the busy highway, not the cars and trucks, only their own wild selves on a deserted road. And I saw myself anew, with all of their agency, driving my own car, joining the wide and moving stream.

PART VI

SPIRIT DRAW NEAR

MADONNA WITH SCARS

Her dark wounded face was everywhere. During my years as a Catholic schoolgirl in the 1950s, statues and pictures of saints on "holy cards" were standard in church, school, and homes but of all these holy people, one stood above and apart. In the community of Polish immigrants in Amsterdam, New York, the scarred face of the Black Madonna of Czestochowa was most beloved, because she alone represented our people's struggle for nationhood.

The Black Madonna painting is said to have been brought to Czestochowa, Poland, by a Hungarian prince, who entrusted her to a group of monks. The monks built a monastery where she still resides, and like many other Black Madonnas throughout the world, she performs the occasional miracle.

The black-robed nuns who were our teachers said her skin was black from years of exposure to candle smoke. I believed that story, and many others they told, until I entered the wider world.

Hussites who fought against the Catholic church attacked the monastery in 1430, slashing her painted face with a sword, but they lost the battle that day. She also gets credit for the retreat of Swedish troops who invaded in 1655. In 1656, the Polish king declared Our Lady of Częstochowa the "Queen of Poland," creating a lasting symbol of national identity at a time when one was sorely needed. In 1920, she again came to the rescue when the Soviet Red Army was about to take Warsaw, only to be defeated after the entire nation prayed to her. During the Communist era, her home in Czestochowa became the center of resistance and her image can still be found in many Polish homes. She is revered as a symbol of solidarity with those who suffer, and for centuries, that was the fate of the people of Poland, land of my ancestors.

But as a young woman in the 1970s, I wanted no part of female suffering. It was the height of the second wave of American feminism. I devoured the words of Betty Freidan, Gloria Steinem, and Adrienne Rich. I was proud of fellow New Yorker and Congressperson Bella Abzug, who joined with Shirley Chisolm and others who founded the National Women's Political Caucus. Feminists advocated for equal rights and responsibilities for both women and men. Being an active, proud woman was fresh and new, and like many back then, I longed to forge my own destiny.

As a girl, I had watched my mother suffer. My father was prone to rages, often bringing her, my sister Judy and me to tears. Once she threatened to leave, frightening Judy.

"She said she was going to pack her suitcase," Judy whispered.

"She won't leave," I said. I knew even then it was an idle promise.

To my mind, the Black Madonna seemed not so much a loving mother as another suffering one. In fact, she was the mother who endured the greatest suffering of all, the loss of her child. My grandmother freely dealt out hugs and kisses, but also urged Mom to "keep the peace." My mother, Lucille, was emotionally distant. I learned passivity at her knee. I know she loved me, but "Get over it" was her most frequent answer to my little girl problems.

Moving into my first apartment, shared with two other girls, was a bold move. I began to learn what assertiveness meant. I moved farther away to college and though

I attended mass every Sunday, I considered other ways to express my spirit. Passive behavior like my mother's was weak in the 1960s. And the Black Madonna was the very picture of passivity.

Then came women's groups with their study of feminine spirituality. I learned that many goddesses were pictured as black, among them Artemis, Isis, Ceres, and Demeter. The gypsies revere St. Sarah, a Black Madonna who is said to have come ashore from Egypt on the southern coast of France in 42 A.D. A servant girl, she is honored by the Roma, people who have known persecution and discrimination.

Riane Eisler, in her book *The Chalice and the Blade,* wrote that if "the central religious figure was a woman giving birth and not a man dying on a cross.. then life and the love of life... and not the fear of death...would be dominant in society as well as art." I quoted her statement in my memoir about growing up suffering, but I have since learned that both life and death are parts of human existence we do well to honor.

My religious school may have gone too far, glorifying pain in song, prayer and visual image- or I may have misinterpreted its intent. In art museum displays of medieval art, I still cringe before the bloody body on the cross. But I also see the value in honoring suffering and using it as a path to empathy and compassion.

Human suffering can lead to solidarity with those who suffer, like the Polish people struggling against oppression. Like abused women like my mom. Like refugees and asylum seekers at our southern border.

An old Polish hymn called Beloved Mother, sung throughout my childhood, especially at funerals, and so excruciatingly slowly I longed for it to end, was, I often said, too much wailing. Now, I'm not so sure. People sometimes need to sing their hearts out. Middle Eastern women ululate, a high-pitched sound of both joy and sorrow, depending on the occasion. It's loud as can be and far from passive.

Drawn to examine this concept, I read more about the Black Madonna, determined to incorporate her into my feminist view of life, and even writing two novels exploring her role in history.

Most women have been scarred, emotionally if not physically. Most of us at times feel unattractive. We use moisturizer and makeup and concealer, covering our scars. But on the Black Madonna of Czestochowa, the scars remain, obvious and visible.

Negative stereotypes of my uneducated ancestors led many to reject their Polish American ethnicity. I felt the scars of "dumb Polack" jokes, and even laughed uneasily, to get along, to be a 'good sport.' But in recent years, I have reclaimed who I am, and with it, the elements the Black Madonna represents. Not just the mourning mother, but the upright, scarred woman who gazes unflinching and steady. She inspires me to straighten my shoulders and walk tall into what remains of my life, embracing the sad with the happy, for both are part of the human story. She is my mother now. Whatever I endure, she is with me always.

LATE BLESSING

I slid a pan of cornbread into the oven and blessed it, like my mother, who made the sign of the cross over every cake, bread and pie she baked.

In middle age, I took up the practice in homage to her and because I could finally do it without cringing. I believed I had put down the heavy load of pain she handed me through a religion I now saw as outmoded and rife with meaningless ritual.

In my eyes, my mother was a long-suffering martyr, verbally abused by my father and devoted to a fantasy of happiness in the hereafter. She read books about saints who endured hideous torture, and quoted their stories to me, her little girl. Suffering earned points with God, and justified staying in a bad marriage. Even then, I didn't buy the message. My friends' parents were loving, their homes quiet and safe, and they went to church too. I thought it should be easy for her to leave and take me with her.

I saw her as cold and uncaring. When a big girl pushed me against a locker in junior high, I came home after school in tears and told my mother. She shook her head for a second in sympathy then told me to get over it and went back to cooking dinner. She had to, after all, live the life she had chosen. I planned my exit every day. I would leave for college and be free and happy, nothing like her.

Although she told me to get over my hurt, I don't think she ever let anything go. No insult was too small to add to her storehouse of suffering. Bitterness colored the stories she told as far back as I remember: My father stood her up when they were dating. Her mother told her to marry him before he changed his mind. He tried to hit her and knocked off her glasses while teaching her to drive. As I listened to her woeful words, I disappeared to myself and became her sounding board, for she had no close friends. Her own mother often told her, albeit in gentle Polish phrases, to calm down.

In the era of women's liberation, I recalled the walk on our knees down the aisle of the church on Holy Thursday to kiss the feet of the crucifix. To me, a young woman now, we were the image of humiliation. I didn't know then that humility has the same root.

Now I bless my bread, knowing there was more to her, each memory another facet to her complexity: Her merry laugh when her brother Johnny told a joke. Her worn hands making me pretty dresses after sewing all day in a factory. The Saturday mornings she led me through five stores to find the right Easter shoes. The grocery list she filled for her elderly mother every Wednesday. And the way, in her own old age, she tried to learn and grow.

She shared her disappointment in her lifelong friend.

"Agnes is so prejudiced. She hates the Puerto Ricans on the East End."

"Didn't you live there when you were kids?"

"Yes, I guess we were the 'spics back then. She just can't see it."

One Christmas Day she made all the food herself. With a full serving dish in each hand, she whispered: "I feel like I'm going to pass out."

"For heaven's sake, sit down."

"I can't."

"It's okay, we love you."

Her eyes filled. Horrified for making her cry, I carried dishes from kitchen to table and cleaned up afterward.

When I was a young wife, I could barely stand to be around her. She was so anxious, so eager to please and so easily cowed. She offered me leftovers to take home.

"If you don't take them, I'll have to throw them away."

"So you're giving me your garbage?" My disdain hit its mark.

I winced at her downcast face, never dreaming I would ever be like her.

Now she is gone, and I know just how hard it is to change. Lifelong habits, even as they hurt us, even as we are aware of that hurt, are easier to continue than to act in a different and completely conscious way. I chase after my grown kids with bags of leftovers as they leave my house. I grab stuffed toys and children's books to entertain my nephew's children, to keep them with me just a few minutes longer, believing those minutes are all I need to make them like me. It doesn't cross my mind that they already like me. Even love me. There is always more for me to do. By myself, without the gifts and the doing, I am never enough.

When my baby cried in his crib, my friend asked if he

liked to be picked up. Yes, I said, staring down at him. When she held him, he turned his head to me.

"He knows your voice."

I didn't believe her.

When he fell, at three, and shrieked in pain, I frantically asked him what happened. His little playmate spoke up.

"Why don't you just give him a hug?"

A smart and easily-bored teenager, he kept his nose in his Game Boy for days, making me look like a bad parent to my friends with high-achieving kids.

"Go outside, call a friend," I said.

A quiet and bookish girl myself, here's what my mother said to me: "Why do you always have your nose in a book? Go outside and make some friends."

She must have felt inadequate. Her child was not popular enough and it was her fault. Now it was mine.

With cornbread in the oven and my apron folded over the back of a chair, I long to take her hand.

"Let's sit," I would say. For just a moment or two, we could step off the treadmill of worry, and stop caring whether we are working hard enough, doing enough, being enough.

God knows, now that I've been all the things I didn't like about her, I understand. It took a lifetime of therapy, meditation, being loved, and actively, consciously loving others who are fraught with worry, just as they are patient with me.

I used to worry about my son. We rarely talked. He clammed up around fifth grade, the year I had major surgery after painful bouts of diverticulitis.

"Who will take care of me if you go in the hospital, too?" he asked his dad.

That same year, my mother was a widow sliding into dementia hundreds of miles away, and I could do little to help her. My marriage hit a rough spot and I criticized my husband at home, not caring to hide it from our son, believing I was sticking up for myself. Unlike my mother.

During those anxious years, I pushed my boy to be more like the active, popular children of my friends. I made him volunteer at the theater and join the track team. At dinner one evening, I snatched a *Left Behind* novel from his hands. What I knew of those books was fear and punishment and not being saved. Judgment and suffering for choosing the wrong faith.

"You're not reading that crap," I said.

He rolled his eyes but did not argue. Now I am haunted by his downcast face. I want to go back and have that helpful parent discussion, the one where I let him read the book and we talk about it, but he's 25 now, and living on his own.

The other day, I pressed his number into the keypad on my cell phone. As before, our conversation had long pauses but I let them be, recalling the long comfortable silences between his father and I when we were dating. When my boy finally spoke, I imagined reaching into the phone, touching him.

"I'm sorry for asking you to repeat yourself. My hearing is getting bad."

"No, it's all right. I was mumbling."

In a long sweet flow of words, he told me about his girlfriend, his work, and his plans to travel. It took a long time for him to say these things, and a long time for me to listen, breathing.

"It was good talking with you," I said.

"Yeah, definitely."

"Love you."

"Love you, too."

Mother Teresa said: "The hunger for love is much more difficult to remove than the hunger for bread."

Before my mother died, I told her about the work I do at my church, where all are welcome. Because I just can't stop going to church.

"You'll have a special place in heaven," she said.

With heat and time, dough rises, transforms into a loaf. The oven timer pings. I open the door to a miracle.

NOTES ON TRANSCENDENCE

Two of my favorite words are "ineffable" and "numinous." I didn't know what they meant until last year. My writing teacher used ineffable often. It means "incapable of being expressed in words." I'm not sure where I got numinous from, but it means "filled with a sense of the presence of divinity." A new word puts a name to a memory.

In 1980, I was newly divorced and driving home from a friend's house. My young son was with his dad for the weekend. At a stop light, I had this thought: "I'm all alone." Another voice in my head said, "I'm here." Now who was that? God? My Higher Self? My guardian angel? The collective unconscious? I don't know, and I really don't need to know. I didn't need to know that night, either. It was ineffable.

When my father was dying in January, 1999, I saw a groundhog. It was late and I couldn't sleep. Sometime in the wee hours, I roamed the little house where I grew up, looking out the windows at the snow-covered yard. The moonlight on the snow was what I'd now call numinous. And into that silent scene came a fat little rodent, scuttling across my old backyard. It stayed there a long time, as if it knew I was watching on this profoundly meaningful night. My mind eased, I went back to sleep.

On another cold winter night, I hurried down a crowded Manhattan sidewalk toward Penn Station. I felt anxious, almost panicky, which is not unusual for me. I felt like a speck in a windstorm, a little fish in a big wide stream. Buffeted by people, and the wind, and tired. Wishing I was home, knowing it would be a couple of hours. And this thought: "I'm always home." Where did that come from? I do believe it's true, but I can't explain it to you, or describe how it calmed my soul.

I'm always home. I sometimes feel I am watched over, cared for by some higher power I call The Benevolent Force.

When I write, I sometimes feel as if the writing is coming "through" me from somewhere else. People call this The Zone or Writing in Flow. I wish it would happen more often.

Philosopher Steve McIntosh, in his book *The Presence of the Infinite,* calls transcendence "a glimpse of something more complete or perfect" than our normal awareness. He believes "we are capable of experiencing spirit more fully and completely as we evolve ...and that these glimpses of the transcendent are a kind of future echo, a foretaste of our destiny as ascendant pilgrims in time."

I love that idea, that we are pilgrims on a journey through time. I love that we try so hard to find our places on that journey. And I love that we are ineffable, numinous pieces of some great mystery we will never fully understand. Most of all, I love that we are trying to figure it out together.

FAITH IN THE FAMILY ROOM

"Mom! Is Jesus God?"

My little boy's voice was high, insistent, rising from the family room where he'd been playing with a friend. I put down my dishtowel and walked down the steps from our kitchen until I could see their little upturned faces. Expectant. Trusting me to give the definitive answer. We attended a congregation where, at Sunday school, he learned about many different faith traditions. We liked to say we embraced the questions. Yet, put on the spot like this, answers were hard to find.

"Well," I began, "lots of people believe ..."

"Yes or no, Mom! Is Jesus God!"

I could have said I didn't know. Maybe I should have. I knew where this had come from. The little neighbor kid, a Catholic, probably told my son that Jesus was God, and my boy had likely disagreed.

Baptized and confirmed, I attended Catholic school through 8th grade. As a group, we professed our belief in God's only begotten Son at every public Mass and often prayed in the classroom. But as an adult, I'd fallen away. And now, it was Easter, a time when literal faith is often put to the test.

I knew that the neighbor boy's parents were devout and sent him to a Catholic school because, his mother once told me, "I want the best for him." I wasn't sure that was the best for my boy. Bad memories of punitive nuns and priests, a focus on the bloody crucifixion and guilt instead of Jesus' life and teachings of love and compassion had long since turned me away.

I've discovered a denomination that professes to search for truth with an open mind. Our minister told me that when an awestruck little boy looked up at him, a big man in long black robes and a bushy black beard, and asked, "Are you God," he said "No, I'm not."

"I wish I had said, 'Yes,'" he told me, "'and so are you.'"

Now it was I being stared at by small and trusting eyes.

I was the one trusted to tell the whole truth. I tried again.

"Some people believe Jesus is God, and many people believe we all have God inside us."

"Yeah!" the little boys shouted, beaming at each other.

Wow, good answer, Mom, I thought to myself. God was inside them both, and all their friends and relations.

When my neighbor came to pick up her little boy, I privately told her about my answer to their question.

"Well, I have my faith," she said, looking away. My statement must have felt like a direct challenge to that faith, and she didn't care to discuss it, which was fine with me. We all have a right to our own beliefs.

Our little boys are now grown, good men both, whose mothers tried hard to ground them in this world of many questions. Last spring, on Good Friday, my neighbor's house had three huge wooden crosses on the front lawn, the crossbeams draped in white cloth. It seems her faith has deepened, and she wants to show it. I get it. Over the years, I have come to understand that Jesus on the cross represents the solidarity of all people who suffer. In other words, all of us.

Is Jesus God? Are we all, in some mysterious way? And

what do we mean by God, anyway? Whatever and whoever she is, I believe she's okay with our questions.

PART VII

SHE WRITES

WHY I STILL WRITE

I was raised to be silent. In boys, in my school and family, loudness was tolerated. Girls were to be quiet, ladylike. Who even uses that word anymore?

I learned my lesson well. A Catholic schoolgirl in the 1950s, I learned that suffering was good and silent suffering ideal. My father and his two brothers were loud, angry men, their wives and daughters cowed, silenced by their ridicule and humiliation.

As a young adult, in high school and college through the 1960s, that vocal decade, people wondered at my silence. Only on the page, writing an essay for class or on a test, did I allow my voice to speak. It surprised a teacher or two who'd thought me dull, mute in all ways since I spoke not a word in class. My eyes were opened

– people *wanted* me to speak, even to be loud (the women's movement helped.)

It was not until my 50s, however, that I turned to writing seriously, beyond my girl's diary and woman's journal. The beginning of that decade was lie someone turned on a faucet in me. I wrote poetry and read it at a church service, even sent it out to be published in tiny periodicals. I read voraciously all my life. Now I had something to say. I wrote essays about my life, found a book – Writing from Life – that led me to SCN, then IWWG. Confident, talented women taught me to craft my raw words and sentences. I began to publish. An editor nominated me for a Pushcart Prize, and a mentor suggested I expand that essay into a book. Three years later, I had gathered memoir pieces and organized them into Off Kilter, and found a small publisher. I was being heard. My friends and family loved the stories I published, but the book was different. I don't know what I expected but the reactions hurt. A cousin said, "You never got over your childhood." (Who does?) "Just because our ancestors had poor communication skills, you didn't have to put them in a book," she ranted. Wife and child abuse is more than "poor communication skills."

Another cousin told me, "it's well-written, but too sad.

Why don't you try fiction? I'm sure it would be just as good."

Yet another was upset that I'd told a secret about her mother from 1939. I wished I'd never shown my book to them, but I never wished I hadn't written it.

Now I'm 63, and time has an urgency to it, it's never had before. I want to say things, write my heart out, be heard. Make a mark. Write. Just write.

CLASS OF REBELS

As soon as I give them the writing prompt, they ask me to read what they've brought from home instead. It's Tuesday afternoon at the assisted living home, and memoir class has begun.

One old guy doesn't like my reading list and rants about Frank McCourt's *Angela's Ashes:* "a thoroughly depressing book." He is very well-spoken and obviously educated though his pointy chin is down near his chest for most of class, exposing his shiny bald head to the fluorescent lights in the ceiling. Some of the students don't hear well, and suggest I use a microphone. They are sitting close together around two long tables but the room itself is large, the ceiling high. I pick up and turn on the mic. A different old gent shouts: "Get that thing out of your mouth!"

I arrange for a smaller room. The "sewing room" is cozy, the ceiling normal height. Before I get two words out, the old gent admonishes me. "Please speak clearly and distinctly."

A woman says her husband can't see due to macular degeneration, so she will do the writing exercises while he sits close and peers over her shoulder. I take him aside and ask if he might use a tape recorder to tell his stories. I say it would make me nervous if someone looked over my shoulder as I wrote. Then I pair him up with the guy who can't hear as they seem to know each other. As I walk away, they are laughing, heads together.

At feedback time, the men in the class are rough on each other but it's all a joke. The women are kind and gentle. One of them says I can be their "leader for life."

During a break, the woman whose husband can't see tells me she feels uncomfortable writing about the black servants she had as a child in the South, because one woman in the class is Black. There are two, I say, but he second woman is very light-skinned, and the old Southerner can't believe it. Didn't she hear the woman read her piece about enslaved ancestors? I tell her I understand but she might want to talk about her feelings with them. She nods and I leave it at that.

They write about what makes them truly happy and come up with an array of themes: being a student, playing sports, the birth of a grandchild, nature, beer, feeling welcome, being comforted, loving family, being alive, and seeing a big city for the first time.

The grouchy old gent asks me how to write "without being verbose." His pieces are so short, I tell him to try to be verbose and it will probably come out just right. I'm not ready to tell him he needs to add some emotion. At the end of class, he says "Please come back."

WRITE ME HOME

The young woman's face on my laptop screen smiled encouragement. Look at the sky if you're near a window, she said, or remember the sky if you are not. Write about what's happening.

I picked up my pen and spiral notebook and wrote about the palest of blues beyond the trees outside my window. I described brown, orange and green leaves clinging to branches. I wrote that I felt as if I were in a bowl of blue, the sunlight to my left a warm beacon.

I did not write about this: My breath was shallow, my body cold and tense. Alone on a solo writing retreat in the Pocono Mountains, I struggled for calm.

I've been anxious all my life. What made me think this was a good idea? The friend who stayed three days in a cabin where her food – and beer – were delivered to her door. A famous writer who checks into a hotel room for days at a time to work on her novel. A friend who drives to her second home in the wilderness to write and canoe alone.

Me, I write at home. I've seen a successful writer at my local Starbucks, laptop keys clicking madly, intent gaze on the screen, coffee cup to one side. I wished I was him, but I just can't focus with people coming and going all around. The only thing I could write about would be the people, their appearance, their manner. I could make up a story, but they'd be gone and new people would walk in and…my keystrokes would stop. My pen and notebook would lay idly by.

When a weeklong stay at a mountain resort came up at our church auction, I made a tentative bid, not sure I wanted to win. It was the only bid. I imagined myself writing and reading all day, stopping only for meals or a walk outside. Maybe even hiking on the nearby trails. But it was gray and cold and miserable the first full day. I walked the hilly roads alone; there was no sidewalk or walking path. Cars passed at low speed but I felt unsafe and vulnerable.

At home, I have the same distractions all writers do: laundry, email, Facebook. Cooking, shopping, the need to exercise. The phone. Anything and everything. I've been trying to complete my second novel for a year. My romantic soul imagined me alone in the mountains with pen or laptop, a cup of tea, and long empty days to pour words onto the page.

Blue, blue, I wrote to the live prompt, inside the bowl of sky. See the blue beauty now, the dancing pink leaves on shrubs near the ground. There is beauty here for me to see, above and below. My frantic attempts to follow instructions yielded trite phrases.

I had the time I said I wanted. And I couldn't breathe. Okay, I could, but I had to concentrate. Deep breath, Linda. In and out.

The online instructor asked us to respond to a quote from Audre Lorde and another from a Whitman poem, with 29 people on a Zoom call. But then they were gone. And the rooms around me were empty.

The crashing loneliness was like a thick blanket threatening to smother me. Where were my inner resources? I've lived seventy years and must have some by now. But I couldn't settle. Journaling about my fear made it worse.

I remembered the cold winter night when I hurried down a crowded Manhattan sidewalk toward Penn Station. I felt scared and anxious, like a speck in a windstorm, a little fish in a big wide stream. Buffeted by people, and the wind, and tired. Wishing I was home, knowing it would be a couple of hours. I remembered the peace of a sudden thought: "I'm always home."

I like being home alone, my favorite things all around me, my trees outside the window, the white noise of traffic on the highway. My cat snoring on the floor beside my desk. But alone on this self-made writer's retreat, I watched the windows and doors.

I tried to make sense of my panicky feelings, researched them on the web, and read about fear of abandonment. I tried hard to work through my anxiety. I told myself I shouldn't feel this way. And then I cut myself a break and went home.

ACKNOWLEDGMENTS

Many thanks to my family and friends who read my work and encouraged me to keep writing once I began to take my craft seriously. Warm lifelong appreciation to the many teachers and mentors who helped me along the way.

The following essays were previously published, sometimes in different form:

Brownie's Mexican Hots, *Inklette, Magazine,* Issue II, April 3, 2016.
Orchid In the Snow, *Wild River Review,* December 2013.
Matters of Fact, *Mocking Owl Roost,* Volume 3, Special Issue 1, February 14, 2023.
The Hartwick College Piano Man, personal blog: www.lindawis.com, June 20, 2022.
Pine Lake, *Ducts,* Issue 20, Winter 2008.
My Grandfather's Ear, *Toasted Cheese,* March 1, 2007.
Lifesaver, *Sky Island Journal,* Issue 23, Winter 2023.
You Have to Eat Lunch, *bioStories,* March 2012.
A Connecting Thread, *Toasted Cheese,* December 2004.

Bread On the Grass, *Hippocampus,* August 2012.

The Darning Egg, *Five Minutes,* February 2024.

Old Women and Other Strangers, *The Sunlight Press,* September 2017.

Walk-In Welcome, *Metropolis,* March 2011.

Bullies, Then and Now, *The Manifest Station,* October 2017.

Danger Boy, *Grown and Flown,* April 2017.

We Came for Toast, *The Sun,* Readers Write, February 2013.

A Lifetime Later, *The Mocking Owl Roost,* Vol. 3, Special Issue 1, February 14, 2023.

This is a Moment of Suffering, *Ginosko Literary Journal,* No. 29, Winter 2022-2023.

Fresh Off the Boat, *Multiplicity Magazine,* June 25, 2020.

Notes from an American Island, *International Human Rights Arts Movement,* Art of Creative Unity Award, 2020. https://humanrightsartmovement.org/notes-from-an-american-island

They Call Themselves Indians, *Little Rose Magazine,* August 23, 2019.

Libretto Decaffeinato, *Story Circle Journal,* December 2023.

Rediscovering the Old Country, *In the Fray,* November 2010.

Thirty-two Words for Peace, *Bookends Review,* July 19, 2023.

Wide Open Spaces, *Ruminate,* Writers Read, fall 2022.
Madonna With Scars, *Story Circle Network* anthology, 2023.
Late Blessing, *Toasted Cheese,* 2016.
Notes On Transcendence, *Ruminate Magazine,* February 2018.
Write Me Home, *Adelaide Literary Magazine,* No. 41, October 2020.
Class of Rebels, *Panoply Literary Magazine,* Summer 2021.

www.ingramcontent.com/pod-product-compliance
Lightning Source LLC
LaVergne TN
LVHW090602110826
845146LV00001B/235

* 9 7 9 8 2 1 8 4 2 4 8 8 6 *